DEMOCRACY
AND DISOBEDIENCE

DEMOCRACY
AND
DISOBEDIENCE

PETER SINGER

CLARENDON PRESS
OXFORD
1973

Oxford University Press, Ely House, London W.1

GLASGOW NEW YORK TORONTO MELBOURNE WELLINGTON
CAPE TOWN IBADAN NAIROBI DAR ES SALAAM LUSAKA ADDIS ABABA
DELHI BOMBAY CALCUTTA MADRAS KARACHI LAHORE DACCA
KUALA LUMPUR SINGAPORE HONG KONG TOKYO

© OXFORD UNIVERSITY PRESS 1973

LC 73-166504

PRINTED IN GREAT BRITAIN
BY RICHARD CLAY (THE CHAUCER PRESS) LTD
BUNGAY, SUFFOLK

PREFACE

In recent years the growth of open disobedience to the law, not by self-seeking criminals, but by people inspired by ideals such as equality, justice, liberty, and peace, has put before us in modern form the ancient philosophical problem of political obligation. Why, or under what conditions and circumstances, ought we to obey the law? This book is intended to be a contribution to the discussion of this problem. My approach is based on the conviction that political philosophy can and should be relevant to issues of current concern. Therefore I make no apology for the fact that my subject is at present a much discussed one.

If philosophers are to say anything of importance about major issues, they must go beyond the neutral analysis of words and concepts which was, until recently, characteristic of contemporary philosophy in Britain and America. Moral and political philosophers must be prepared to give their opinions, with supporting arguments, on the rights and wrongs of complex disputes. This is what I have done in this book. One inevitable consequence of this approach is that disagreement must be expected. It would not be true to say that I do not mind whether people disagree with my views, for this would imply that I think my own views no better than any opposed views—in which case it would not have been worth while putting my own views forward. What I can say, however, is that I have tried to put my views forward not as dogmatic assertions, but on the basis of arguments; and if the arguments are shown to be unsound, or better arguments are produced in favour of alternative positions, then clearly the views I have argued for will have to be abandoned.

As the subject of this book is one that concerns not only those studying or teaching political philosophy in universities but also any citizens, especially citizens of a democracy, who find themselves faced with a law they oppose, I have tried throughout to write in a way that can easily be understood by those who have never studied philosophy. Accordingly professional philosophers will have to be patient if I occasionally elaborate points with which they are familiar. Non-philosophers will not, I hope, find difficulty with anything, except possibly some parts of the Introduction. Anyone who does find these passages difficult will do best to skip them.

One more point about reading this book that I want to make at the outset is that the book should be read as a whole. Although Part I contains the core of my arguments, anyone who reads this part without reading the qualifications and amplifications contained in the second and third parts will receive a quite misleading impression of my views and the direction of my arguments. The reader is asked, therefore, to reserve his judgement until the end.

This book began life as a thesis, submitted to the University of Oxford in 1971 in partial fulfilment of the requirements of the degree of Bachelor of Philosophy. My thanks go to my supervisor, Professor R. M. Hare, not only for his careful point-by-point criticisms of early drafts, but also for his encouragement of what was, in some respects, an unorthodox university thesis. Others who read later stages of the typescript, and to whom I am indebted for comments and criticism, were Professor H. J. McCloskey, John Dwyer, and Christine Swanton. In addition, I must thank my students in political philosophy over the past year, with whom I have had many useful discussions on the issues dealt with in this book.

Finally, I dedicate this book to my parents who will, I trust, see it as a worthwhile product of my long absence from home.

Oxford,
September 1972.   PETER SINGER

CONTENTS

PART III

INTRODUCTION

I T is not difficult for most of us to imagine situations in which we would be uncertain whether we ought, morally, to obey a particular law. I shall not give examples now, as different people may be uncertain about different cases, but the reader can probably think of a case himself easily enough. In deciding how one ought to act in such a case, a variety of considerations will be relevant. One consideration which many people have thought to be important is the nature of the system of government from which the law derives. It is often asserted that if this system is democratic, this will make a crucial difference to the question of whether to obey. It is frequently said—especially by leaders of governments that are generally considered democratic—that while disobedience may be justifiable under certain political systems, for instance, Nazi or Communist dictatorships, it is never or almost never justifiable in a democracy. One could quote many statements expressing this idea. The following example is from a speech by a former Prime Minister of Australia, at a time when there was widespread disobedience in opposition to the presence of Australian troops in South Vietnam:

As to inciting people to break the law, I think there can be no excuse whatsoever for those in a community where the opportunity exists to change the law through the ballot box.[1]

There is respectable philosophical support for this view. T. H.

[1] *The Australian*, 27 Aug. 1970, p. 1, from a speech by the Rt. Hon. J. G. Gorton. For a similar view expressed by Mr. Q. Hogg, when Shadow Minister for Home Affairs, see *The Times*, 18 Feb. 1970, p. 3; see also G. Kennan, *Democracy and the Student Left* (Hutchinson, London, 1968), pp. 15, 166–7.

Green, for example, said this about the problem of obedience:

Supposing then the individual to have decided that some command of a 'political superior' is not for the common good, how ought he to act in regard to it? In a country like ours, with a popular government and settled methods of enacting and repealing laws, the answer of common sense is simple and sufficient. He should do all he can by legal methods to get the command cancelled, but till it is cancelled, he should conform to it.[1]

The aim of this book is to examine the view represented by these quotations, that is, the view that whether or not a system of government is democratic vitally affects our obligation to obey laws emanating from that system. Before commencing this examination, however, there are some unavoidable preliminaries.

Firstly, I must say something about the framework within which the following discussion is to take place. I have just written of 'our obligation to obey laws'. I must therefore explain what I mean by 'obligation', and in particular, my understanding of the nature of political obligation.

There are various kinds of obligation. One relatively straightforward kind is legal obligation. I am, under the laws of the United Kingdom, legally obliged to refrain from assaulting other people. There is a valid law which says I must not do so, a law certain to be upheld by the highest court of the United Kingdom if I should be misguided enough to challenge it. Moral obligation is more controversial. There is no settled procedure for determining what moral obligations we have. According to their different moral opinions, people think we have moral obligations to do and refrain from doing different things. In general, though, people say that we have moral obligations to do things like pay our debts, help those in distress, refrain from using violence except in self-defence,

[1] T. H. Green, *Lectures on the Principles of Political Obligation* (Longmans, London, 1907), sect. 100, p. 111.

oppose genocide, keep promises, avoid damaging natural eco-
logical systems, and so on. Not everyone will agree that we
have moral obligations to do all of these things, but most would
agree that some of them are obligatory, especially if I add that,
as I shall explain shortly, by 'obligatory' I do not mean
absolutely obligatory whatever the circumstances may be.

Our ultimate obligation to obey the law is a moral obligation
and not a legal obligation. It cannot be a legal obligation, for this
would lead to an infinite regress—since legal obligations derive
from laws, there would have to be a law that says we must obey
the law. What obligation would there then be to obey this law?
If legal obligation, then there would have to be another law . . .
and so on. If there is any obligation to obey the law it must,
ultimately, be a moral obligation.

What is the force of 'moral' when I refer to these obligations
as 'moral obligations' and distinguish them from legal obligations? The definition of 'moral' is a topic which has so pre-
occupied moral philosophers in recent years that they seem to
have forgotten that talk about definition should be only a
preliminary to the discussion of more substantial ethical
problems. In order to avoid this pitfall, I will simply say that
as I shall use the term 'moral' a person acts according to moral
considerations whenever he acts on considerations which he
would be prepared to apply universally, and which are, for
him, more important than any other similarly universal
considerations.[1] By 'considerations which he would be pre-

[1] In saying this, I take a position similar to that of R. M. Hare, *Freedom
and Reason* (Clarendon Press, Oxford, 1963), esp. ch. 2. This is hardly the
place for an extended discussion of Hare's position, but I think that by
regarding a man's moral principles as those principles which are overriding for him among the principles he is prepared to universalize (this
qualification is important, for it makes explicit the idea that a man could
regard selfish, non-universalizable and hence non-moral principles as
overriding) we can avoid many of the difficulties which some critics have
found in Hare's analysis. For my own views on the problem of defining

pared to apply universally' I do not mean that moral principles must be very general principles, like 'Thou shalt not kill', which are supposed to apply in all possible circumstances. Rather, I mean that one must be prepared to apply moral principles without regard to the particular individuals affected by them, the result of this requirement being the separation of moral principles from purely selfish principles, which cannot be universalized. The man who says that all law-breakers should be severely punished but, when his own tax fraud comes to light, maintains that he ought not to be punished at all, is not judging morally, for he does not apply his own principle to himself. Making exceptions for oneself involves failing to apply one's principles universally.

There are, of course, universal considerations which people may act on which are not moral principles. Considerations of aesthetics or etiquette are examples. This is why a second part of what I mean by morality is that it is more important than any other universal considerations. Generally, we think morality more important than aesthetics or etiquette. Indeed, if someone consistently treated aesthetic considerations as more important than those considerations we normally think of as moral—if, for instance, an artist were to sacrifice his family for the sake of his work—we might well say that, for him, art was the first principle of his morality. I think, though, that this element of importance is less central to the notion of morality than the element of universal applicability.

That is all I shall say about the meaning of 'morality'. If the reader disagrees, or is puzzled by what I have said, he will probably do better to read on than to reread the last two paragraphs. However difficult it may be to set out briefly, I do

morality, see my article 'The Triviality of the Debate Over "Is-ought" and the Definition of "Moral" ', *American Philosophical Quarterly*, vol. 10, no. 1 (Jan. 1973).

not think that the way I use the term 'moral' in the remainder of this book will cause much difficulty.

Political obligation I take to be a form of moral obligation. Some people have denied this, maintaining that political obligation and moral obligation are separate and equal species of the genus 'obligation'.[1] This seems obviously wrong to me, but I need not argue this point because as I have defined 'moral', political obligation must either be a form of moral obligation or else subordinate to it. (To be strictly accurate, it could be based on self-interest, in which case it would not be a form of moral obligation, but this is not the sense of political obligation which raises interesting theoretical questions. There is very little that can be said in general terms about whether it is in one's interest to obey the law.) Political obligations, then, are those moral obligations which are peculiarly associated with forms of political organization. They are the moral obligations which one would not have, were it not for certain facts about the nature of a community or group of which one is a member. This definition, again, I leave vague, for 'political', like 'moral', is easier to understand than to define.

Having said that political obligation is a form of moral obligation, and having said what I mean by 'moral', I have still to say why I am talking about 'obligations', rather than about reasons for acting, or simply about what we ought to do. The language of obligation seems to assume a special view of morality. Utilitarians, for example, might prefer to talk solely in terms of doing whatever has the best consequences, without reference to 'obligations' arising from past undertakings or relationships. So, instead of talking of a moral obligation to obey the law, wouldn't it be better to talk of moral reasons for obeying the law? Often, I think, it will be better to talk of

[1] e.g. T. McPherson, *Political Obligation* (Routledge, London, 1967), esp. ch. 8; T. D. Weldon, *The Vocabulary of Politics* (Penguin Books, Harmondsworth, 1953), pp. 56–7.

moral reasons rather than obligations. Even though our concern is with what is usually known as the problem of political obligation, this does not compel us to deal with obligations rather than reasons. In places, however, I shall use the language of obligation. When I do so, I hope it will be in a way that is compatible with any moral position, utilitarian or not. But in order to explain the way in which I shall discuss moral issues, I need to sketch the context of the argument of this book, or, in other words, my view of the state of the discussion to which it is intended to contribute.

Writers on political obligation used to put the question with which they were concerned as: 'Why ought I to obey the law?' Now the tendency is to ask, rather, 'When ought I to obey the law?' Since the Nuremberg trials, and the events which gave rise to these trials, we have become acutely aware that the obligation to obey the law does not apply to all laws in all circumstances. There is now no need to discuss whether it is *ever* right for a citizen to break a law of his society. We have even, I think, got beyond arguing whether it is ever right to break the law in a democracy. Could anyone plausibly maintain that if the Nazis had received majorities in free elections, and allowed freedom of speech, association, and so on, this would have made it right to obey laws designed to exterminate Jews? To maintain this would require fantastic, and surely misguided, devotion to democratic laws. It is true that the passages I quoted on the first two pages of this book seem to take this position, but no doubt if the authors of these passages were pressed they would admit that there could be circumstances under which it would be right to break even a democratic law.[1]

---

[1] Green did in fact say that disobedience to the United States Fugitive Slave Laws would be justifiable, although he seems to have had no doubts about the United States being a democracy. (Op. Cit.. sect. 144–7, pp. 149–53.)

Alternatively, one might defend the position that it is never justifiable

I shall assume that whatever reasons there are for obeying the law in any society, there may be stronger reasons against doing so in particular cases. In other words, our political obligations are not absolute. In trying to decide whether to obey the law in different cases, we are faced with conflicting considerations. If we continue to talk of an 'obligation' to obey the law it must be understood that by this is meant, not an absolute obligation, but rather an obligation to which some weight is to be given. Obligations of this sort have usefully been termed *prima facie* obligations, and I shall sometimes use this term. It is, I think, a notion familiar to most people. When I promise to meet someone at a particular time I put myself under an obligation, but it is not an absolute obligation. The obligation would be overridden if, for instance, a neighbour asked me to drive his expectant wife to hospital. On the other hand, the obligation is not negligible, and it would be wrong of me to break it because at the time I preferred browsing in a bookshop.

Our discussion of political obligation is concerned with conflicting moral considerations which will be of some weight, but will not be absolute or overriding. The aim of this study is to try to sort out some of these considerations, and ascertain which of them hold and under what conditions. This task is an indispensable preliminary to reaching a decision in particular circumstances about whether or not one ought to obey a law.

---

to break the law in a democracy by saying that democracy is incompatible with the persecution of minorities, so that any government which attempted to commit Nazi-like atrocities would not be a democracy. (See P. Bachrach, *The Theory of Democratic Elitism* (Athlone Press, London, 1969), pp. 19–20.) I would not want to define 'democracy' so widely, but in any case the point is a purely verbal one, and the example can be altered to avoid it—the point I am making would be the same if genocide were aimed, not at a minority within the democratic system, but at people in another country.

Although such a decision depends too much on individual circumstances for me to be able to say in precisely what circumstances one ought or ought not to obey a law, I hope that what I have to say will, by providing a framework into which particular facts can be fitted, make it a little easier to come to a rational decision about whether to obey.

I shall describe the process of resolving conflicting moral reasons for acting into a decision as 'balancing' or 'weighing up' the conflicting reasons. This description is intended only as a helpful metaphor. It is not to be taken as implying that moral problems are solved by intuition, by 'seeing' that an act is right, or by any other particular method. I hope that my terminology will be acceptable to those who hold a wide range of moral views, and a wide range of philosophical and not-so-philosophical positions about the nature of morality. Nothing I shall say, I hope, will assume either the truth or the falsity of any of the following views: that there are objective moral truths, that moral language has no other function than to express a certain kind of feeling or emotion, that morality derives ultimately from God, that morality is a purely human invention, that we learn what we ought to do by intuiting the basic principles of morality, that we ought always to do whatever act will promote the greatest possible balance of happiness over misery, or that we ought to be concerned above all else to act justly. There are, of course, many other moral positions, too many to mention, with which my approach would be equally compatible, and also some extreme positions with which it would be incompatible. I have already, by my definition of 'moral', excluded anyone who thinks morality is compatible with having no concern for anyone's interests but his own. I must also exclude those who think that reason and argument have no role to play in morality—those who think we must intuit, in each specific situation and without the help of any general principles at all, what we must do; or those who think we must make a non-rational commitment to some course of action, without even intuiting anything. I cannot argue in a way that is relevant to those who hold this kind of position, because argument itself is irrelevant to them. I shall try, however, to write so as to presuppose very little, apart from the assertion implicit in any discussion of a moral issue, that reason and argument are relevant to moral decisions.

To this end, I shall write mainly of 'moral reasons' for and against doing something. When the moral reasons are of the special sort we normally refer to as 'obligations', that is, when they are created by a voluntary act of the person obliged, and the act is owed to other specifiable people, I shall describe them as obligations. Any utilitarian, or anyone else who dislikes this term, may construe it as a short-hand way of referring to particular kinds of utilitarian reasons. Throughout, the utilitarian may regard any general principles for which I argue as similar to rules about keeping promises and telling the truth, that is, as rules of thumb, guides to utility which are useful when, as is often the case when disobedience is contemplated, utilities and disutilities cannot be calculated with any precision.

There is now little more to say before we can turn to our subject-matter itself. I shall not give any special definition to terms such as 'disobedience' and 'democracy'. I must point out, however, that by the former I do not necessarily mean just 'civil disobedience' (though the meaning of this term is in any case controversial).[1] I am concerned with moral considerations relevant to most, if not all, acts or omissions to act which the agent believes would be held to be illegal by the highest court in the country. I shall mostly have in mind acts which are

[1] Some examples of the numerous varying definitions which have been offered can be found in H. A. Bedau, *Civil Disobedience: Theory and Practice* (Pegasus, New York, 1969), pp. 218–19.

public or become known to the public, rather than acts which the agent intends shall remain secret, such as illegal abortions. I am also concerned with acts motivated by broad political and ultimately moral considerations, rather than purely selfish acts, but I shall try to indicate at what points the particular nature of the act makes a significant difference to its moral standing.

I am not in general concerned with acts of disobedience to a law which the agent hopes will or would be declared to be an invalid law when or if it is examined by the highest authority in the country's legal system. Much of the campaign against segregation laws in the American South falls into this category. At least in some cases, the aim of the disobedience was to test whether the laws that were disobeyed were constitutional, in the not unreasonable hope that they would be declared unconstitutional. I exclude this kind of action from consideration because it raises issues fundamentally different from those raised by acts which are violations of laws, the legal validity of which is unchallenged. One can engage in acts designed to test a law without regarding one's acts as disobedience, and without doubting that one has an obligation to obey all valid laws.[1] I am interested in acts which claim to be justified irrespective of what is valid law.

So much for 'disobedience'. The other key term of my title

---

[1] Admittedly the division between the two kinds of action is not as easy to draw as might at first appear. It is blurred, and perhaps rightly, by those who insist, against the legal positivists, that even within existing legal systems, the morality of a law is relevant to the question of whether that law is a valid law. This is why I have said that the dissenter must believe that his act of disobedience would be held to be illegal by the highest court of the country, and not said simply that he must believe his act to be illegal. On this issue see R. M. Dworkin, 'Is Law a System of Rules?', in A. Summers (ed.), *Essays in Legal Philosophy* (Blackwell, Oxford, 1968), and 'On Not Prosecuting Civil Disobedience', *New York Review of Books*, 6 June 1968.

I shall leave even more open at this stage. The meaning of 'democracy', as it relates to the obligation to obey the law, will be discussed in the course of the book.

With this, our preliminaries are complete. We may now begin our examination of the claim that there are stronger reasons for obeying the law in a democratic society than there are in any other form of society.

PART I

DEMOCRATIC AND NON-DEMOCRATIC MODELS COMPARED

OUR purpose is to examine the reasons for obeying the law which may exist in democratic and non-democratic societies, to see if there are any significant reasons which hold in the one but not the other. In order to compare and contrast these different forms of society, I am going to use some simplified models. The use of simplified models as a basis for political theory has been criticized. It is true that simplified models, just because they are simplified, fail to bring out all the complexities of actual political situations. Yet they may still be useful in helping us to see something that is obscure in a more complex situation. One of the main objections to the use of models to illustrate problems of political obligation in particular is that the models chosen are usually voluntary associations, or associations with definite, specified purposes, while actual political societies are involuntary associations without definite or specified purposes. My models will at least avoid these obvious pitfalls.

THE MODELS

I take as my basic model a common-room association of a university college, similar to those at Oxford. At Oxford colleges, the Junior Common Room is the political body of all the undergraduate students. It functions in a manner similar to student unions at many other universities. Because of its small size, however, and because it is easier for members to meet together in a residential college, it suits my purposes slightly better than a students' union at a large, non-residential university would. The accuracy of my account as an account of how Oxford common-room associations function is, of course, immaterial. I will just stipulate that the following facts hold, and the reader can regard the model as a purely hypothetical construct. The relevant facts, then, are these. Membership of the common-room association is automatic for all members of the college. Subscriptions to the association are taken from college fees, so one can withdraw from the association only by withdrawing from the college altogether. This would be highly inconvenient, and to withdraw from one college without joining another is, we shall say, out of the question. Any other college to which one went would have a similar common-room association to which one would also have to belong. The common-room association has been in existence for as long as anyone can remember, and if any records of its origin ever existed, they have been lost. So none of the members knows how the association was originally set up, or for what purposes. Every member simply found the association in existence when he joined the college.

This is the basic model. I will now describe three variants of it. Consider first an association in which all the important decisions about what the association shall do, how its money be spent, and so on, are made by one man, known as the Leader. The origin of this particular system is to be found in the immediate past history of the common-room association. Some time ago, the man who is now the Leader claimed that the decision-procedure then operating had led to stupid decisions, not in the real interests of the association. Henceforth, he would make all the decisions himself, guided by the interests of the members. If anyone objected, they were invited to fight it out with the Leader's friends, who were the best fighters in the association. No one objected. Since taking power, the Leader's decisions have accorded reasonably well with his promise to rule in the interests of all.

One of the tasks which the association has carried out for as long as anyone can remember is the selection of a number of newspapers for the common room, to be paid for from general funds, and read by whoever wants to read them. So that all may read these papers, there is a regulation that no one is to remove papers from the common room until they have been there for a week. One day, the Leader decides that the common room should subscribe to a new paper, which I shall call *The News*. A member of the college, who will be called the Dissenter, objects to the newspaper, not for personal or aesthetic reasons, but because the paper carries out a scurrilous campaign against the minority of black people in the country, implying that blacks are always dirty, lazy, and dishonest, and should not be allowed to mix with whites. This campaign, we shall say, manages to keep within the bounds of the law. The Dissenter finds the very presence of the paper in the common-room offensive; he also fears that if other common-room members, less aware than he is of the paper's bias and distortion, read the paper regularly, it will inflame latent prejudices and they will come to discriminate against the two or three black members of the college. (Once again, whether this would really happen is not relevant for our purposes; if the reader finds the example implausible he can substitute one of his own. It would not matter if the Dissenter's objection to *The News* was on the grounds of obscenity, or because it was a propaganda sheet for the armed forces.)

The Dissenter asks the Leader to reconsider his decision, but the Leader is unmoved. The Dissenter then decides to take stronger action. He goes into the common-room every morning, before the other members are about, and removes the paper.

For comparison, consider now two common-room associations similar to the above in every respect, except for the methods of taking decisions. Firstly, consider an association in which decisions are still made by one man, but he did not have to seize power, and he does not have to intimidate opponents with threats of violence. In this association there has been a tradition, for as long as can be remembered, that the person who has been a member of the college for the longest time— the Senior Member—makes all the decisions (there is a recognized method for determining who of those who entered in the same year is the most senior). The Senior Member is expected to decide in the interests of all, and it is, again, reasonable to claim that he does so.

As in the first association, the decision to subscribe to *The News* is taken, the Dissenter vainly puts his case to the Senior Member, and finally resorts to removing the paper.

In the final association, the custom is and, so far as is known, always has been, for decisions to be taken by a vote of the whole association at a general meeting, the majority view prevailing. The Dissenter attends these meetings, and votes according to his opinions. Sometimes motions which he favours are carried, sometimes they are lost. When a motion is carried, those who voted against it accept it, and do not hinder its being put into effect, although they may try to get the decision changed at subsequent meetings. At the meetings, all members are free to speak, subject only to some necessary procedural restrictions. The meetings are conducted fairly, and the votes tallied accurately.

At one meeting, it is proposed that the association take out a subscription to *The News*. The Dissenter argues against this proposal, but fails to carry the majority with him, and the motion is passed. At the next and following meetings, he attempts to get this decision rescinded, but fails again, and it becomes obvious to him that a majority of the members have made up their minds firmly in favour of the paper, so that he will not be able to sway them, or at least, not before the paper has been in the common-room long enough to bring about the deterioration in racial harmony which the Dissenter fears. On realizing this, the Dissenter removes the paper as before.

The question which I want to ask about these models is not whether the Dissenter was justified in breaking the regulation against removing newspapers—to answer this we would need further information on, among other things, the probability of serious harm resulting from members reading *The News*, and whether simply removing the paper was likely to be effective in the long run. I want to ask if, on the facts as we have them, there are any differences in the weight of the moral reasons against removing the paper in each case. In all three models, the action was contrary to a rule of the association. If there is a special reason (or reasons) for obeying laws in a democracy, we should be able to detect reasons for obeying this rule of the association in the third case which do not hold in the other two.

There are several reasons for obeying laws which apply more or less equally to all three models. Any act of disobedience may set an example, which could lead to others disobeying. Widespread disobedience could mean a breakdown of 'law and order'. 'Law and order' may be a catch-cry which conservatives are prone to use for electioneering purposes, and as an excuse for stifling legitimate opposition, but it is, I think, indisputable that law and order are generally desirable, and that a society in which there was constant disorder would find it difficult to achieve the elementary benefits which co-operation and security make possible. Even an anarchist's utopia would have some settled and generally accepted principles of co-operation and administration. In all three model societies, as I have described them, there are settled and accepted principles and procedures of this sort. In so far as any act of disobedience might lead to a general disregard of these principles and procedures, this is a consideration against disobedience to be taken into account in all three models. It does not give us any special reason for obedience in the third model which does not hold in the other two.

Another argument for obedience which applies equally in all three situations is that the members of the association have all benefited from previous decisions reached through the decision-procedure of the association, and from the fact that other members have obeyed these decisions. Thus the Dissenter has, we may assume, benefited from the fact that a variety of newspapers is available in the common room, and that they have not been removed by other members. The fact that one has received benefits from the laws of a society has long been thought to be an important reason for obeying the laws. This argument is used by Socrates in Plato's *Crito* when he rejects the suggestion that he should escape from prison. Once again, though, it is an argument which has no special application to the third model. Since decisions made by non-democratic procedures may benefit one as much as decisions made by democratic procedures, the argument applies wherever there is benefit. In describing the models, I specified that in all three, decisions had for the most part been made in accordance with the interests of members.

It might be objected, though, that whatever stipulations I made in setting out the models, it is in fact much less likely that decisions made by one man would be in the interests off all than that decisions made collectively by all the members of the association would be. In fact, I think the most that can be said is that decisions made collectively by all the members of the association are more likely to be in the interests of a majority—not all—of the association. If it is held that one man is very likely to act selfishly if he has the power to make decisions for all, then it should also follow that a majority of the members, given the same power, is likely to put its interests before the interests of the minority. Thus, if the 'benefits received' argument is said to be unlikely to apply when there is rule by one person, it must also be said that it is unlikely to apply to everyone even when there is collective decision-making. But we need not go further into this problem at this point. I shall be saying more about the problem of minorities later on. The point I want to make now is that even if it is true that most democracies make laws in the interests of all, whereas few non-democracies do, this does not mean that the fact that one is living in a democracy is, in itself, a reason for obeying the law. It means only that the 'benefits received' argument for obedience is more likely to apply. It remains possible that there are democracies in which it does not apply, and dictatorships in which it does. Finally, it seems to me doubtful whether the argument has any relevance when the disobedience is not intended to benefit oneself (as it would have in Socrates' case) but other people, perhaps not even members of one's own society, to whom some wrong is being done.

There are also a host of more minor arguments for obedience which apply to all or most societies, irrespective of the nature of the political system in operation. For instance, there is the fact that disobedience usually leads to the expenditure of public resources in the prevention or limiting of disobedience, and the enforcement of the law against those who disobey. These resources could have been better spent in other ways. Whatever the significance of the reasons, major and minor, for obeying any settled form of government which rules in the interests of all, I shall not be discussing them. As our focus is on the difference between democratic and non-democratic societies, I shall concentrate on reasons for obeying the law which may mark a significant difference between democratic and non-democratic societies. My procedure will be to look for reasons for obedience which may apply to the third model, but not to the other two. At this stage of our inquiry I shall regard the third model as a model of a democratic society, and the other two as non-democratic. This is nothing more than a device to enable me to tackle different issues one at a time; I hope no one will be misled into thinking that anything I say applies straightforwardly to those nations we commonly refer to as 'democracies'. The important question of the extent to which the conclusions reached from a consideration of the three models apply to actual societies and systems of government is discussed in the third part of this book.

THE POSSIBILITY OF REPEAL

In the passage I quoted at the outset of this book, T. H. Green mentioned two features of 'a country like ours' which he apparently thought sufficient to oblige a man to obey a law even though he believes it is not for the common good. These features are 'popular government' and 'settled methods of enacting and repealing laws'. Are these peculiarly strong reasons for obeying laws, applicable only in a democracy?

I will take first the reason to which the Australian Prime Minister also referred, in his statement of a position like that of T. H. Green—the possibility of 'change through the ballot boxes'. Strictly speaking, there is nothing specifically democratic about having settled methods of enacting and repealing laws—all sorts of non-democratic procedures for doing this can be imagined. What Green no doubt meant, however, and what Gorton meant too, is that in a democracy the individual citizen can attempt by legal means to get a law changed. In the third model association this is provided for by the possibility of moving at any meeting that a decision of a previous meeting be rescinded. Does this constitute a significant reason for obeying a decision to which one is opposed?

In describing the course of the dispute between the Dissenter and the majority of the members of the third association, I specified that after the initial decision to order *The News*, the Dissenter tried to get the decision rescinded, but failed, and became convinced that he would not be able to prevent members reading the paper by such means, or at least, not until it would be too late to prevent the harm he feared. This means that the possibility of legal change in the near future is no more than a theoretical possibility. The possibility of legal change in the distant future may be slightly more real, but it can be discounted, since the object of the change is not to get the decision rescinded for its own sake, but to prevent specific harm which may well by then have occurred.

If the Dissenter is right in believing that there is no practical possibility of changing the decision to which he objects by legal means and before the harm he is concerned to prevent has occurred, can a purely theoretical possibility constitute a significant reason for obedience? We can clarify this question by imagining that a legal process has been instituted in the first or second model—for instance, the presentation of petitions to the Leader or Senior Member—which provides for a theoretical possibility of changing a decision. It may be objected that the possibility of legal change by means of petitioning an autocrat is less real than that which exists in a democracy, no matter how large the majority against one's proposals. Legal change through petitions is at the sole discretion of the autocrat; in a democracy change must result if the majority favour it. Nevertheless, the possibility of changing by legal means a decision in any of the three models depends upon changing the opinion of one or more persons. When a meeting of the third association decides by a very narrow majority, it may not be too difficult to change the decision—but the same would apply when an autocrat has difficulty in making up his mind on an issue. When a meeting of the third association decides by a large majority of members, all or nearly all of whom are convinced that their decision is the right one, the possibility of change by legal means is every bit as theoretical as the possibility of changing the decision of a firmly resolved Leader or Senior Member by means of a petition.

It seems to me, therefore, to be a mistake to regard those possibilities of legal change which necessarily exist in a democracy as a significant reason for obeying the law. Only when there is a real possiblity of legal change before the harm one seeks to prevent has occurred, is this possibility an important reason for using only legal means to bring about change in a law. The strength or importance of the reason then would seem to be in direct proportion to the reality of the possibility of bringing about change by legal means. But because one cannot be sure whether there is a real possibility of legal change until one has tried, I think the existence of a theoretical possibility does constitute a strong reason for attempting to use legal means first, and resorting to illegal means only if the attempt fails.

Perhaps I should also say here that I do not deny that the theoretical possibility of legal change by majority vote is essential for the existence of democracy, and it may therefore be a necessary condition of some other reason for obedience to law, deriving from the existence of a democratic form of government. I have argued only that it is not, in itself, an important reason for obeying the law.

POPULAR SOVEREIGNTY AND CONSENT

The other reason for obeying a bad law in a democracy mentioned by T. H. Green was simply 'popular government'. The meaning of this term is not quite clear, but we may take it that Green was referring to what is better known as 'popular sovereignty', which expresses the idea that the government is in some way a government of the people. This is still vague, and it is in any case difficult to know exactly what to make of the claim that the existence of popular sovereignty is an important reason for obedience. The point is not, one supposes, that the laws of a popular government are always or nearly always the best laws possible. It is surely beyond dispute that popular governments can make mistakes, as can any other form of government. It is more likely that those who talk of the importance of popular sovereignty have in mind the idea that only a popular government can have legitimate authority.

Unfortunately, the commonly invoked notion of legitimate, rightful, or lawful government is not a helpful one. When is a government legitimate? 'Legitimacy' sounds as if it were a quality or characteristic which some governments have and others do not have, but if we try to say what this quality or characteristic is, we find it difficult to agree. Often when a person refers to a particular government as legitimate, he is doing no more than expressing his support for it, or giving his allegiance to it. In this case, the term 'legitimate' refers to no quality or characteristic at all. It does not describe anything.[1] A person who says 'The only legitimate form of government is government by the people' must be taken to be saying that he will not support or give his allegiance to any form of government except 'government by the people'. This suggests that we may be able to avoid the difficulties raised by the notion of legitimacy by by-passing that notion, and going directly to the proposed criteria for legitimate government. After all, even if we could make sense of the claim that we ought to obey those governments which are legitimate, we would still have to produce reasons for holding that certain forms of government are legitimate while others are not. So there seems to be some

[1] On this, see R. M. Hare, 'The Lawful Government', in P. Laslett and W. Runciman (eds.), *Philosophy, Politics and Society* (third series, Blackwell, Oxford, 1967).

advantage, and no disadvantage, in going directly to these reasons, instead of via the notion of legitimacy.

Starting from the claim that we ought to obey a government because it is popular, we came to the further claim that such governments ought to be obeyed because they derive their authority from the people. 'The people', though, is a term which includes ourselves, if we are citizens of the government. We are therefore likely to ask what basis there is for asserting this derivation of authority. The standard answer, the answer of the American Declaration of Independence, of Locke, Rousseau, and innumerable others, is some theory of consent. A popular government is one which, as the Declaration of Independence says, derives its just powers from the consent of the governed. Its citizens ought to obey it because they have consented to its rule. On this view, the obligation to obey the law is similar to the obligation to keep a promise.

To many readers the consent theory of obligation will be familiar ground, and I must apologize for taking them over it once more. The usefulness of doing so will emerge only later. I intend to test the consent theory of obligation by seeing how it applies to our three model associations. Have the members of any of the associations consented to the method of government of their association? Does the third association differ from the other two in this respect?

In the first model, the Leader retained power with the assistance of his friends, the best fighters in the association, who threatened to fight anyone who objected to the rule of the Leader. Consent under intimidation—or rather, acquiescence under intimidation—is all that exists here, and this could not satisfy a consent theorist, for it could not give rise to the sort of moral obligation required.

A comparison between the second and third models is more interesting. In both, physical intimidation is absent. In one case, there is general acquiescence in the rule of the Senior

Member (at least, there was until the Dissenter decided to disobey). In the other, the Dissenter and most of the other members went to the meetings at which decisions were taken, and participated in them by voting. What conclusions can be drawn from these facts? It will be recalled that common to all three models was the fact that no one ever agreed to join the association, or to accept any particular decision-procedure. There was no knowledge of any original agreement, or of any agreement to set up any particular method of making decisions. So express consent by the members to any form of government is absent in all three models.

In the absence of express consent, supporters of the view that consent is a crucial reason for obeying the law have argued for the existence of tacit consent. It has been argued that simply by remaining a member of a society one tacitly consents to be bound by its laws. So, someone might say, since the Dissenter has not left the association, he has tacitly consented to be bound by its decision-procedure. But in our model associations it was, for practical purposes, impossible to quit an association without entering another association which would also have a system of government which one would have to obey. This counts heavily against taking mere acquiescence to a form of government, as in the second model, as a sign of consent. Consent, to give rise to obligations, must be voluntary, and this means that there must be some alternative to consenting. The only alternative to acquiescing was disobeying, which is what the Dissenter is now doing.

Even in the third model, although there is active and voluntary participation in the decision-procedure, this cannot be taken as proof that there is real consent to the decision-procedure. The Dissenter (and other voters) may feel that since decisions will be taken whether he votes or not, he may as well make the best of things by doing what he can to improve the chances of a good decision being reached. This sort of attitude does not involve actual consent to the method of making decisions by majority vote. So we cannot urge the Dissenter to obey this decision-procedure because it really has the consent —either express or tacit—of the governed. The Dissenter is governed, but may not have consented. This much is true of all three model associations, notwithstanding the important differences between them.

EQUALITY AND FAIRNESS

Realizing that consent will not do, many who regard democratic government as peculiarly worthy of obedience have pointed to other aspects of 'popular sovereignty'. It has been argued that all men have an equal right to govern themselves, and that for this reason we ought to obey only those forms of government in which all men have an equal share. This belief has played an important role in liberal and democratic thought. It is, ultimately, either an assertion or a prescription for which it is very difficult, if not impossible, to argue. It is hard to do anything but accept or reject it. Taken as an assertion, it cannot be finally refuted, since no matter what respects men are shown to differ in—wealth, intelligence, height, benevolence, or any others—it can always be said that these are not relevant to having an equal right to govern oneself. It also cannot be finally established, since the respects in which men are said to be equal, and which are said to be relevant to the equal right to govern, are usually intangibles about which differences are possible—for example, equal dignity, equal moral worth, or equal original freedom.

It might be said that the fact that almost everyone agrees that children do not have the right to take part in government shows that there are criteria for deciding who has this right which we all can recognize in practice. Quite apart from the fact that the consensus on the exclusion of children is no longer as rock-solid as it once was, however, this point can give little comfort to the egalitarian. For if the exclusion of children from government can be justified, it must be on the grounds that children lack certain characteristics which adults possess. These characteristics might be something like knowledge of the issues involved in making decisions, or ability to reach a responsible judgement. But adults differ in these respects too, so if it is right to exclude children for lacking these characteristics, it should also be right to exclude some adults, or, at the other end of the scale, to give multiple votes to those who possess these characteristics to an above average degree. (This latter proposal, incidentally, was supported by no less a democrat than John Stuart Mill.[1]) If, despite this, we do believe in the equal rights of adults to govern, it must be, as I have already suggested, on the basis of less tangible characteristics.

Another suggested basis for equality is that it is enough to show that there is some characteristic, which all men possess, such that once one has the characteristic, the degree to which one has it is irrelevant. To take a parallel, all points inside a circle possess the characteristic of being inside the circle, and no point possesses this characteristic to a greater degree than any other point. Now is there some similar characteristic which is relevant to the equality of men? John Rawls, in his book *A Theory of Justice* says there is. It is, he says, the capacity for moral personality.[2] Although it seems to me that this kind of approach is more likely to meet with success than the search for some characteristic which everyone possesses to an equal degree, it will still not convince people unsympathetic to the notion of equality. 'Why should mere capacity for moral personality be decisive?' they will ask, 'why not the degree to which a person's moral personality actually has developed?' Or

[1] J. S. Mill, *Representative Government* (Dent, London, 1960), ch. 8.
[2] J. Rawls, *A Theory of Justice* (Clarendon Press, Oxford, 1972), sect. 77.

why make moral personality decisive at all, rather than something like knowledge, intelligence, or experience? Once again, the only possible replies take us into the realm of assertion and counter-assertion rather than argument.

In the current political climate these difficulties in establishing the basis of equality are likely to seem mere academic quibbling. Hardly anyone argues seriously for a hierarchical society now. No one proposes depriving people of the vote because they are ill-informed or unintelligent. In these circumstances the need for a sound basis for equality will not appear pressing, but the absence of a sound basis could be unpleasant if the political climate should change, as it did in the 1930s. This is why it is unfortunate that, so far as I can see, a really satisfactory basis is yet to be produced.

Quite apart from the difficulty of proving the original assertion (or justifying the original prescription), however, equality is not a completely satisfactory basis for explaining why we ought to obey the law in a democracy. For the assumption or prescription can be turned against the purpose for which it is being used. It can be taken as showing, not that there is a special obligation to obey democratic authority, but that there can be no obligation to obey any authority except oneself. In other words, it may be denied that the equal rights of all to govern themselves are satisfied by majority government over the minority. What reason is there for supposing that 'equal rights' can be added up in such a way that the side with more has the right to prevail over the side with less? Equal rights to a cake would not be satisfied if the majority walked off with the whole cake. So even if it be accepted that all men have equal rights to govern themselves, more argument is needed before it can be concluded that a system of government like that of the third model association has a valid claim to be obeyed which other systems do not have.[1]

[1] For a related argument, see the passages from H. D. Thoreau

We can avoid some of the difficulties just discussed by arguing simply that the decision-procedure of the third association is fairer than those of the other associations. In support of this position we can make use of the generally accepted proposition that fairness requires an equal division, unless there is a sufficient reason for alloting more to some than to others. Since the decision-procedure of the third association does divide power equally, in that every member has one vote, and the other decision-procedures do not, there is a *prima facie* case for saying that only the decision-procedure of the third association is fair.

Predictably, we run into trouble as soon as we try to make this *prima facie* case absolute. How are we to establish that having been in the college longer than anyone else is not a sufficient reason for having more decision-making power than anyone else? This has to be established if claims that the decision-procedure of the second association is fair are to be refuted. There is a tendency among writers living in Western democracies to assume that, at least under normal conditions, a democratic system is the fairest way to divide power; but if this assumption is not made, the contention is very difficult to prove. The Senior Member might claim, in support of his system, that his longer experience made it possible for him to make better decisions, in the interests of all the members, than could be reached by any more egalitarian method. This is not a matter that can be satisfactorily settled by abstract argument. We can point out, to any Senior Member who claims that his position is fair, that if he is to hold this view, he must be prepared to hold it even if it should be discovered that not he, but some other member to whose views he is strongly opposed has in fact been a member of the college longer than he himself has

quoted on pp. 40–1 and 94, and the discussion which follows the quotations.

been.[1] If we are honest with ourselves, this may make many of us realize that we cannot regard any non-democratic system as fair, at least under normal circumstances; but it is possible to hold the opposite view without any inconsistency. At this point, therefore, I must rather lamely leave it to the reader to decide for himself if the decision-procedure of the third association is fairer, and therefore has a better claim to allegiance, than the decision-procedures of the other associations. I will go on to consider another way in which the decision-procedure of the third association may be fairer than that of the other two. This argument takes as its basic assumption the point at which the argument just considered was halted—the difficulty of establishing what is to count as a sufficient reason for having more than an equal share in the making of decisions.

FAIRNESS AND COMPROMISE

We have seen that although the decision-making power in the second model association is unequally distributed, the Senior Member can still contend that it is fairly distributed, because there is adequate reason for him to have complete power. Now in the dispute over *The News*, the Dissenter's action (removing the paper) is an attempt to assume complete power in respect of whether members of the association shall read the paper. Like the Senior Member, the Dissenter can claim that there is good reason for him to exercise more than an equal share of power over this issue—because, say, he is the only member of the association fully aware of the harmful tendencies of the paper. The Dissenter could put forward this justification of his action in all three model associations. In the first two

[1] This is an application of the principle of universalizability mentioned in the Introduction. For a parallel argument, see R. M. Hare, *Freedom and Reason* (Clarendon Press, Oxford, 1963), ch. 6.

associations, it is a claim against the claims of the Leader and Senior Member. In the third association, where the decision-making power is evenly distributed, the Dissenter's claim is against all the other members. His claim will be challenged by other members who, having voted in favour of subscribing to the paper, will consider him to be mistaken about its harmful tendencies, or perhaps about the importance of these tendencies. The Dissenter, after all, is acting on his own judgement about this. The other members have their own judgements too, which they sincerely believe correct. In claiming that his own judgement entitles him to a greater say in the matter than the others, the Dissenter is making a claim which the others could make, and which, if many of them did make, would be incompatible with the continued existence of a peaceful decision-procedure.

A difference between the models can now be seen. Assuming that agreement on the merits of the competing claims cannot be reached, the nature of the decision-procedure in the first and second associations gives the Dissenter no valid reason for abandoning his claim to decide the issue, and accepting the claim of the Leader or Senior Member. (I mean by this, no reason arising out of the nature of the decision-procedure. There would of course be the usual reasons, some of which I mentioned earlier, which apply to almost any decision-procedure.) In the third association, on the other hand, the Dissenter does have a valid reason, arising from the nature of the decision-procedure, for refraining from acting on his own judgement. If the Dissenter believes the other members to be sincere in their opinions about *The News*, and accepts the impossibility of reaching agreement on the issue, he will be able to see that on this and similarly controversial issues, it would be best if everyone were to accept some sort of compromise, instead of acting on their own individual judgements. The Dissenter thus has a reason for supporting and accepting such a compromise—but he, like everyone else, will want to retain as much influence on decisions as is compatible with such a compromise. He will not want to be at a disadvantage.

The decision-procedure of the third association, in which all members have equal say in decisions, and then accept the result, is a paradigm of a fair compromise. It is, obviously, a beneficial compromise, since a peaceful settlement of disputes is better than settlement by force. The benefit of peaceful settlement would, however, also be achieved if everyone accepted any other decision-procedure. The distinction between the associations is that it is only in the third association that the nature of the decision-procedure makes it possible for everyone to refrain from acting on his own judgement about particular issues without giving up more than the theoretical minimum which it is essential for everyone to give up in order to achieve the benefits of a peaceful solution to disputes. It is the fairness of the compromise by which force is avoided that gives rise to the stronger reason for accepting the decision-procedure of the third association. This may seem a strange thing to say, since I have previously argued that abstract discussion cannot prove the third system to be fairer than the second. My point depends upon a distinction between 'absolute fairness' and the kind of fairness which is limited by what can be achieved in a given situation—or as I shall call it, perhaps rather loosely, 'fairness as a compromise'.

When we say that an arrangement is fair, we often mean not that it is absolutely fair, but that it is fair given the conditions under which the arrangement is made. These conditions may include a certain amount of ignorance, or a lack of agreement in a situation in which agreement is essential. For example, if we were called upon to judge between two claimants to a sum of money, and after hearing both sides we were of the opinion that although the claims were incompatible, there was no way of telling which was the better, we might think it fair to divide the money between the two. If the claims were to something which could not be divided, we might toss a coin to decide. Under the circumstances, this would be a fair compromise, although from the point of view of one who had 'absolute' knowledge, and thus knew which of the claimants was entitled to the money, it could be said to be unfair because it gives as much to the party who deserves none as to the party who deserves all.

For a different example, in which a compromise is required not so much because of ignorance as to what is absolutely fair, as because of the need to come to some agreement, we might take a dispute between husband and wife as to who should get up when the baby cries at night. The wife may say that the husband should get up, because she attends to the baby all day, while the husband feels that the wife should get up, since he has worked all day. They both feel, equally strongly, that their own position is correct. Agreement on the merits of the matter cannot be reached, but some agreement is essential, since neither wants the baby to cry unattended. A fair compromise under these circumstances would be for the husband and wife to take it in turns in getting up. This is a compromise because both parties give up some part of what they claim, in order to reach an agreement which is even more important than having their own way on the particular issue. There could, of course, be other compromise solutions. If the husband were, in the last resort, prepared to let the baby cry all night, while the wife were not, she might have to settle for some other arrangement, for instance, that she would get up every week-night, and the husband only at weekends. This would still be a compromise— both parties are still giving up something—but it would no longer be a fair compromise. The unequal arrangement is not based on any recognition that the husband's case is the better one. It is based merely on the greater strength of his position.

I hope that these examples have made the notion of 'fairness as a compromise' reasonably clear. When the merits of incompatible claims cannot be ascertained, or when agreement on the merits of such claims cannot be reached, a procedure like tossing a coin, or dividing what is in dispute equally, is the fairest course that can be taken. It is generally to be preferred to allowing superior force to settle the issue.

It should be obvious from what has been said before that a society which disagrees fundamentally over the kind of decision-procedure it should have is in a state appropriate for fair compromise. The various incompatible claims that are being made cannot be settled by rational argument, nor is it likely that they can be settled by any decision-procedure, since it is precisely the decision-procedure that is in dispute. As the Italian anarchist Errico Malatesta once argued:

If you choose 100 partisans of dictatorship, you will discover that each of the hundred believes himself capable of being, if not sole dictator, at least of assisting very materially in the dictatorial government. The dictators would be those who, by one means or another, succeeded in imposing themselves on society. And, in course of time, all their energy would inevitably be employed in defending themselves against the attacks of their adversaries . . .[1]

Malatesta thought that this was a reason against having any government at all; it seems to me that it counts at least as strongly in favour of the obvious compromise solution of giving everyone an equal voice in decisions, and if we think that, men being what they are, some government is preferable to no government, we will prefer a fair compromise solution to the anarchist solution.

As a further illustration of the need for compromise, consider the fate of the proposal made by John Stuart Mill, which I have already mentioned, that while everyone should have at least one vote, those with superior education and intelligence should have additional votes. As Mill himself said, later in life,

[1] E. Malatesta, *Anarchy* (Freedom Press, London, 7th ed., 1942), p. 35

this was a proposal which found favour with no one. The reason, I think, is not that it would obviously be unfair to give more votes to better qualified people, but rather that it would be impossible to get everyone to agree on who was to have the extra votes. Mill seems to have believed that the uneducated would accept the claims of the educated, and agree that education was a proper qualification for having a greater voice in decisions. Yet even now, when everyone has one vote, there are frequent complaints about 'pointy-headed intellectuals' who think they know better than ordinary men how the country should be run. Assuming that we did believe Mill's system of voting to be perfectly fair, it would still be a brave, or rather a foolhardy, man who would put it forward as a serious proposal. In view of the row such a proposal would stir up, it would be wise to put aside beliefs about what is perfectly fair, and settle for the sort of compromise represented by 'one man, one vote'.

The decision procedure of the third association, then, is a fair compromise between the competing claims to determine what the association shall do, because it gives no advantage to any of the parties to the dispute. (It would be more accurate to say: it gives no inbuilt advantages. It may give an advantage to a particularly persuasive speaker, but this is an incidental and probably minor factor. If this were felt to prejudice the fairness of the compromise, however, it would be possible to avoid it, at some cost, by allowing chance to determine who shall take decisions, in rotation. The ancient Greeks used this method. Our disinclination to do so is probably based on the feeling that the incidental unfairness involved in a system like that of the third association does not justify the presumably inferior decisions that would be the result of distributing power by lot.) As a fair compromise, it is greatly preferable to a 'fight to the finish' over each controversial issue. Fairness as a compromise is all that can be expected because, as we have seen, it is extraordinarily difficult to decide—let alone to reach agreement on—what is a sufficient reason for an unequal distribution of power.

The point I am making can also be seen as a point about the different implications of a resort to force in different situations. The Dissenter, in removing *The News*, is resorting to force against the decision-procedure of his association, no matter what that decision-procedure is. But the position he takes in respect of the use of force is importantly different in the third model. Disobedience to a system which is a fair compromise implies willingness to impose one's own views on the association. It is an attempt to gain, by force, greater say than others have about what should be done (or, in the case of disobedience intended not to affect a particular issue, but to lead to the overthrow of the decision-procedure in operation and its replacement by some other decision-procedure, an attempt to have greater say about what sort of decision-procedure there is to be). This is not necessarily true of disobedience to a decision in which the Dissenter was denied the participation that he would have had under a fair compromise. In the first and second associations, disobedience is compatible with willingness to accept a fair compromise whereby one's own views have no more influence than those of anyone else. When there is no fair compromise, one can disobey in order to obtain a decision-procedure which does represent a fair compromise. To disobey when there already is a fair compromise in operation is necessarily to deprive others of the say they have under such a compromise. To do so is to leave the others with no remedy but the use of force in their turn.

What all this amounts to is that there are strong reasons for playing one's part in supporting and preserving a decision-procedure which represents a fair compromise. To disobey under these circumstances is to reject the compromise and to attempt to use force to impose one's views on others. There is much less justification for asking the Dissenter to obey in an association like the second model, in which there is a peaceful decision-procedure but no fair compromise. It is true that disobedience could lead to a breakdown of the peaceful decision-procedure here too, but it need not involve any greater an imposition of one person's will upon the other members than exists prior to the disobedience. Moreover, to ask the Dissenter to obey in such an association is to ask him to give up his claim to power completely, without any reciprocal concession from the other party to the dispute.

I hope that this is a reason for obedience that can be accepted by people who hold a wide variety of moral views. Utilitarians can accept it, because I have been arguing that, in general, there is a greater danger of undesirable consequences if one disobeys a decision-procedure which represents a fair compromise than if one disobeys one which does not. For the utilitarian this may be only a very rough guide to conduct, but even a rough guide is better than no guide. Those who are not utilitarians may consider that considerations of fairness or justice are additional reasons for supporting a fair compromise when no fairer outcome can be reached.

Perhaps to prevent misunderstanding I should state explicitly that my argument is not of the form: 'If everyone disobeyed the decision-procedure would collapse, therefore you should not disobey.' The difficulty with this form of argument is that everything hangs on the degree of precision with which we specify what it is that we are doing.[1] If everyone disobeyed whenever they disliked any decision, of course the decision-procedure would collapse. The Dissenter will say, however, that he disobeys only when there has been a flagrantly and seriously mistaken decision, and he may think that the decision-procedure would be improved if everyone did that.

[1] What follows is a highly abbreviated version of an argument developed by D. Lyons in his book *Forms and Limits of Utilitarianism* (Clarendon Press, Oxford, 1965).

The Dissenter may even say that he disobeys when there is a flagrantly and seriously mistaken decision, *and* no one or hardly anyone else is disobeying at all. If everyone disobeyed only in precisely these circumstances, the Dissenter can argue, the decision-procedure could not possibly collapse. In this way, and quite justifiably, the Dissenter may describe his act so that all its causal consequences are included in the description. Then, when we ask: 'What if everyone did as you are doing?' the answer turns out to be identical with the actual result of the Dissenter's action. So this form of argument breaks down into straightforward utilitarianism.

If the 'fair compromise' argument I have given can be accepted by a utilitarian, it may be thought that it must depend on the actual consequences of disobedience, so that it is only if disobedience is really likely to lead to the breakdown of the fair compromise that the reason for obedience given will have any weight. This line of thought is based on a false model of the way political arrangements in general, or decision-procedures in particular, rise and fall. It imagines that there is some definite percentage or number of acts of disobedience which is necessary and sufficient to bring about the downfall of a decision-procedure, and that if this quota is not reached, any acts of disobedience will be quite ineffective so far as the stability of the decision-procedure is concerned. The model is that of an election—if the candidate does not get a majority, any votes cast for him are of no effect, while if he does get a majority, any votes over the bare number necessary to get him elected are equally ineffective. But political institutions are not like this (nor, as utilitarians have pointed out, are social institutions like promising). Their strength and stability depends on the support they get. No doubt there is some small amount of disobedience which any reasonably stable system can take without incurring an appreciable risk of breakdown, but once this small amount has been passed, any further disobedience will make a direct contribution to the likelihood of a breakdown of the decision-procedure. The situation here is like that which occurs when pedestrians on a heavily-used route have the option of taking a short-cut across a lawn, or going a longer way round. A few can take the shorter route without the lawn suffering any damage, but once a certain number regularly do so, any further increase in numbers makes a real contribution to the deterioration of the lawn into a mud-patch.[1] Moreover, while under certain circumstances people may be able to cross lawns when no one else is around, and so avoid setting an example which will increase the damage, most forms of politically motivated disobedience must, to fulfil their purpose, be public or at least become known. The possibility of a breakdown is therefore a factor for a utilitarian to take into account, and while the contribution of a single act of disobedience, even including the example set to others, may be minute, the disastrous consequences of a breakdown of the decision-procedure may be so bad as to give that minute contribution considerable significance.

It would also be a mistake for a utilitarian to assume that the only undesirable consequences of disobedience my argument points to are those associated with the possibility of a complete breakdown of the decision-procedure. The utilitarian considering disobedience must also take into account the fact that his act of disobedience, against a decision which he considers to be bad, but others consider good, may lead some of the others to disobey a decision which the Dissenter thinks good. Thus, to return to our specific example, the Dissenter, in removing *The News*, must bear in mind the chances of his act inspiring someone else to remove a magazine, say, *Peace News*, which the Dissenter thinks excellent, but others consider a dangerous subversive influence. Even if there were to be no more disobedience after these two incidents, the loss of *Peace*

[1] This is what D. Lyons calls a 'threshold', op. cit., pp. 71–3.

News might in itself counterbalance the gains from the removal of *The News*. In the first and second models, one can suggest, as a way out of this 'tit for tat' situation, a decision-procedure that is a fair compromise; in the third model, this option does not exist, since those who disobey have, by their conduct, rejected it. This is a further utilitarian reason why disobedience is more serious in the third model. There is a greater risk, not only of 'total war', but also of light skirmishes, because there is no obvious basis for a peace agreement.

We have been inquiring whether the fact that a government is 'popular' should be a reason for obeying it, and if so, why. The answer I have given is not new. If I had to reduce it to one sentence, I could not do better than the old epigram about democracy being a method of government which counts heads instead of cracking them (or replaces bullets by ballots, as a more modern pundit has put it). I have tried to show why this is an important reason for obeying a government like that of the third model association, and why it is inapplicable to the other models, even if the Leader and Senior Member do manage to rule without cracking heads.

Although not new, the reason for obedience for which I have argued may be in need of re-emphasis. It tends to be given little importance by many writers on democracy, perhaps because it is not as high-sounding as some of the reasons we had to reject. The notion of a compromise, many people seem to feel, is somehow degrading, and incompatible with the idea of acting according to moral principle. This is a feeling which finds expression in some anti-democratic writing of both the Right and the Left. An example is the following passage from the essay 'Civil Disobedience' by the nineteenth-century American radical, Henry Thoreau:

All voting is a sort of gaming, like checkers or backgammon, with a slight moral tinge to it, a playing with right and wrong, with moral questions; and betting naturally accompanies it. The character of the voters is not staked. I cast my vote, perchance as I think right; but I am not vitally concerned that that right should prevail. I am willing to leave it to the majority. Its obligation, therefore, never exceeds that of expediency. Even voting *for the right* is *doing* nothing for it. It is only expressing to men feebly your desire that it should prevail. A wise man will not leave the right to the mercy of chance, nor wish it to prevail through the power of the majority.[1]

Now in a sense it is true that accepting the fair compromise decision-procedure is a kind of gaming, and that the obligation to do so can never exceed that of expediency. One may feel that on some issues the result which emerges from the ballot boxes is so monstrous that one cannot possibly accept it, even if it is the outcome of a fair compromise. In this way one might consider it imperative to do more for what one thinks right than merely vote for it. I have not denied this, for I said at the outset that I was seeking to establish obligations which are not absolute, moral reasons to be taken into account, rather than moral reasons which ought to prevail in all possible circumstances. But while I grant that there is this amount of truth in what Thoreau says, I cannot accept the implication that it is wrong to engage in the gamble of voting, and that the obligation of expediency is unworthy of serious consideration by men concerned to do what is right. If the alternative to accepting this form of gaming is a resort to force, a resort which is likely to be bloody, and is no more likely to produce the result one considers right than the fair compromise decision-procedure, I would say that that is an excellent moral reason for accepting the fair compromise. Whereas Thoreau opposes doing what is right to 'leaving it to the majority', I would say that in most cases, if a fair compromise in operating, there will be no difference between these apparently alternative courses of action.

[1] H. D. Thoreau, 'Civil Disobedience'. First published 1849, reprinted in H. A. Bedau (ed.), *Civil Disobedience: Theory and Practice* (Pegasus, New York, 1969), p. 32. Italics in original. I discuss Thoreau's views more fully on pp. 94–6.

THE PROBLEM OF MINORITIES

I have argued that a system like that of the third model association, in which every member has a vote, is a fair compromise. To this an important objection can be made. It is best put by means of a hypothetical example. Assume that in our third association there is a minority of people who are marked off from the other members in some way—let us say, they are blacks, while the majority are white. Over a period of time, and at various general meetings, decisions are taken which put the black members at a disadvantage. For example, at one meeting it is proposed that black members should not occupy armchairs when doing so leads to a white member having to sit on one of the less comfortable benches. The blacks vote against this proposal, but it is carried. The same happens with other proposals, and when at subsequent meetings the blacks attempt to get the decisions rescinded, they are consistently outvoted by the solid white majority. Surely all this makes the decision-procedure no more than a travesty of a fair compromise.

The objection must be accepted. In the circumstances described, it is clear that the fact that each member has an equal vote is insufficient to ensure that the system operates as a fair compromise between all parties. Analysis of the notion of fairness helps us to see why this is so. In discussing the fairness of the position of the Senior Member in the second association, I have already referred to the principle of equality in a minimal or formal sense. In considering whether a decision can be applied universally, one puts oneself in the position of everyone affected by the decision, like interests counting alike, no matter who the person affected happens to be. It follows that in order to hold that an arrangement is morally justifiable, one must be prepared to hold that any other arrangement which does not differ from the first arrangement, except in respect of the position particular individuals occupy in the arrangement, would also be justifiable. This means that white members would have to be prepared to accept the arrangement even under the imaginary condition that their own skins should suddenly turn black. In the circumstances described, assuming that no significant facts have been omitted, it is clear beyond reasonable doubt that the white majority cannot sincerely hold that their treatment of the black majority is justifiable. The way the whites are treating the blacks can properly be said to be unfair.

Members of an association who are treated unfairly have less reason for obeying the decision-procedure of the association that they would if they were treated fairly. To be more specific, if negative: they do not have the reason *for* obedience which they would have if the system did operate as a fair compromise. But it is important to determine the exact significance of this point. If this is not done, mistaken practical conclusions could be drawn.

When we say that a decision-procedure is and operates as a fair compromise, this cannot mean that every decision will be a fair compromise. What it does mean is that there will be no tendency or general pattern of decisions which are unfair to a particular group. In other words, while some decisions may be unfair to one group, and others unfair to another group, different groups will be disadvantaged by different decisions, so that, taking a long-term view, there will be a 'fair distribution of unfairness'. The obvious question this raises is: how many unfair decisions are needed before the conclusion that the system is operating unfairly can be drawn? I think this depends on circumstances. One ought to take into account not just the decisions themselves, but also facts about the community. If there is a history of prejudice towards a group, manifested not just in decisions but also in speeches by politicians, or common attitudes, it will be much easier to conclude that there is unfairness than if there is no such history. The actual application of the criteria for a fairly operating system, however, must be a matter of judgement in each case.[1]

This raises a further problem. At any time, in every large society, there are likely to be a number of groups who believe that they are being treated unfairly. As well as ethnic minorities, there will be socio-economic groups. In the United Kingdom, the moderate Catholics of Northern Ireland are an example of an ethnic group which claims it has received unfair treatment over a long period of time. (I exclude the more extreme Catholics, as well as the Welsh and Scottish nationalist movements, as they seem to be demanding independence rather than fair treatment.) Farmers are a socio-economic group, some of whom, at least, also believe they are not being treated fairly. Both these groups have committed acts of civil disobedience in support of their causes. Farmers have stalled farm vehicles in busy streets, and Northern Ireland's Catholics have withheld rent and rates, as well as staging protest marches. There are many other groups which may feel they have good grounds for disobedience because they have been consistently put at a disadvantage by political decisions. If it is a matter of judgement in each case whether the group is being treated unfairly, and we leave this judgement to the group concerned, there seems to be a danger that the reason for obedience for which I argued will lose whatever weight it has, since there are so many groups which will consider that as they are unfairly treated by the decision-procedure, they are not at all obliged to obey it. This would make it difficult to settle issues involving the interests of these groups by institutional means. Yet to leave the judgement about when a group is being treated unfairly to the majority, or to any body ultimately under the control of the majority, is impossible for the obvious reason that the majority would then be judge in its own case.

[1] For an example of such a judgement, see the Appendix.

There is no solution to this problem. The decision to be made is about when the decision-procedure is functioning properly, and hence cannot be left to the decision-procedure. So it must be left to the group concerned, and we must hope that the criteria I have outlined are sufficiently clear to prevent too many wrong decisions. The most that can be suggested as a safeguard is the creation of a 'buffer zone' by the stipulation that the unfairness in the operation of the system must be 'unmistakably clear' (or some similar requirement). If this were observed, there might be a few cases of really unfair decisions which, because the unfairness was not sufficiently clear, were obeyed when disobedience would have been justified, but there would be a substantial gain in social peace.

In the light of this discussion, I must modify the conclusion of my previous argument. We can still say that the fact that a system of government operates as a fair compromise between competing claims to power is a major reason for obeying that system, but we must now emphasize the importance of the system not merely being a fair one, but operating fairly as well, in that the majority does not use its votes to the constant disadvantage of the minority. If 'popular government' just means that the government derives its powers equally from all the people, this alone is not quite sufficient to give rise to the reasons for obedience for which I have argued.

PARTICIPATION

I shall now consider the significance of another feature to be found in the third model, but not the others, which I believe adds to the reason for obedience just discussed. First I should note, however, that the fact that a decision-procedure is a fair compromise gives the Dissenter a reason, not just for obeying the decision, but also for participating in the decision-procedure. We saw that the essence of the fair compromise was that everyone gives up his own claim to have more than an equal say in deciding issues, but retains his claim to have an equal say. In that way every member can have the maximum influence compatible with a peaceful settlement. In order to have this influence, the Dissenter must participate in the decision-procedure. Because the decision-procedure is a fair compromise, the Dissenter ought to try to influence decisions through the decision-procedure, rather than by some other method incompatible with it.

In the description of the third association it was specified that in discussions and votes over issues which had arisen prior to the question of the subscription to *The News*, other members of the association had accepted and obeyed decisions of the association to which they had been opposed, but which the Dissenter had supported. Behaviour like this, I shall argue, gives rise to a *prima facie* obligation on the Dissenter to accept the decision of the association over *The News*, a decision which other members favour, but to which he is opposed. Indeed, I think it can be seen that the obligation does not depend on the fact that the Dissenter happens to have been, on previous occasions, on the majority side. Rather, the Dissenter incurs the obligation when he participates in the decision-procedure together with other members who are opposed to the Dissenter's views, but prepared to accept and obey whatever decision the majority should favour. (I call this an obligation and not a moral reason because, as is typically the case with obligations, it is created by the voluntary act of the person obliged, and is owed to other people.)

This obligation is not necessarily peculiar to decisions made by a democratic procedure. It is like the obligation to abide by the ruling of an umpire, when one has led others to believe that one would do so, and when they are prepared to accept the umpire's verdict, however it goes. Thus if, in a dispute between two members of any one of the three associations, someone had suggested submitting the dispute to the decision of the Leader, Senior Member, or assembled members, as the case may be; and if both disputing parties had then argued their cases before the Leader, Senior Member, or assembled members, there would be an obligation on the loser to accept the verdict of the decision-procedure. This obligation would be the same in all three cases. Normally, however, decisions in the first and second associations are not reached by these means, and there is no conduct by any of the members of the association which can be said to give rise to reasonable expectations that he will accept the verdict. In the third association, on the other hand, all decisions on which there is any dissent are in a sense decisions on disputes between parties, and the participation of the Dissenter in the decision-making process can be said to give rise to reasonable expectations which will be disappointed by his refusal to accept the verdict of the majority.

I argued earlier that participation in the democratic process need not imply actual consent to the results of that process. By likening the obligation to accept a majority verdict to the obligation to accept the verdict of an umpire, however, I may now have given the impression that I have reintroduced consent. It is therefore important to see how the obligation for which I am arguing differs from consent-based obligations, at least on one plausible interpretation of the meaning of 'consent'.

The obligation for which I am arguing depends on the fact that under certain circumstances, actions or failures to act may justify us in holding a person to be obliged *as if* he had consented, whether or not he actually has. I shall call this 'quasi-consent', the prefix indicating that it is not real consent, but gives rise to obligations as if there were real consent. (Compare the legal notion of 'quasi-contract', defined by a legal dictionary as 'an obligation not created by, but similar to that created by contract, and independent of the consent of the person bound'.)[1]

Quasi-consent is obviously different from express consent; it is also, I think, distinct from the idea of tacit consent which has been invoked by many of the writers who have wanted to make consent the basis of the obligation to obey the government. If we read what Locke, probably the best-known of these writers, said about consent, it seems that even though he held that there could be consent which was not expressed in any way, he still thought of this tacit consent as a mental act, a 'saying in one's heart' which differed from express consent only in that it was not said aloud. So, according to Locke:

. . . every man that hath possession of any part of the dominions of any government doth thereby give his tacit consent, and is as far forth obliged to obedience to the laws of that government during this enjoyment, as anyone under it, whether this possession be of land to him and his heirs forever, or a lodging for only a week; or whether it be barely travelling freely on the highway . . .[2]

Admittedly, the meaning of this passage is not altogether clear, but on one interpretation it is easy to distinguish Locke's tacit consent from quasi-consent. This interpretation is clearly put by J. P. Plamenatz:

Locke assumes that a man by merely travelling within the territories of the King of England *actually*, though *tacitly*, agrees to obey his laws. It follows then that a journey in England constitutes a promise to obey the King's laws. The promise is tacit because it is not expressed in words, orally or in writing, but it is none the less a promise. The word 'tacit' cannot alter the nature of the consent; it can only indicate the manner of its expression. Either there has been consent or there has not. Locke believes that there has.[3]

[1] P. G. Osborn, *A Concise Legal Dictionary* (Sweet and Maxwell, London, 5th ed. 1964).

[2] J. Locke, *Second Treatise on Civil Government*, par. 119.

[3] J. P. Plamenatz, *Consent, Freedom and Political Obligation* (O.U.P., Oxford, 2nd ed., 1968), p. 7.

Tacit consent, then, is a form of actual consent. The consent exists, as it does in express consent. This is at least a plausible interpretation of Locke. I am not concerned to argue that it is the correct interpretation. It has been, at any rate, the basis for several refutations of Locke's theory of obligation, including that of Plamenatz. My concern is to make clear the distinction between what, on my view, is involved in participation in a decision-procedure, and this notion of tacit consent. If there are other interpretations of Locke which render 'tacit consent' in such a way as to make it similar or equivalent to what I mean by quasi-consent, this does not matter, so long as it is understood that by quasi-consent, I do not mean that there is any actual consent.

There are circumstances in which behaviour may give rise to an obligation to act as if there were consent, even when there is no actual consent. For example, a group of people may go out for a few drinks. One member of the group buys the first round of drinks for everyone, then a second member does the same, and so on in turn. If, after most members of the group have done this, one member, who has accepted drinks paid for by the others, refuses to buy anyone else a drink, he will be thought to have behaved badly. One could say that he has an obligation to buy the others a drink. The obligation does not arise from actually consenting to buy drinks, for the man may never have agreed to do so, either expressly or to himself. He may even have intended all along to have a few drinks at the expense of other people. Yet by acting in a particular way, one may become involved in an obligation to which it is no defence to say: 'I never consented.' Not consenting is not enough. Some positive act expressing one's non-consent would be necessary. If the drinker had said something like: 'I'll accept drinks if you offer them to me, but don't think that because I do, I am going to buy anyone else a drink', he could have avoided the obligation which otherwise falls on him.

The ground of the obligation for which I am arguing is that the Dissenter, by voluntarily participating in the vote on the question of whether *The News* should be ordered, understanding that the purpose of the election is to enable the group to reach a decision on this issue, has behaved in such a way as to lead people reasonably to believe that he was accepting the democratic process as a suitable means of settling the issue. Whether or not he actually, or 'inwardly' consented to this decision-procedure, he cannot now be heard to say that he never accepted the validity of the election. After the election it is too late to say that one never accepted its validity. Others participated in the election in good faith. They would have accepted the result if it had gone against them. For the sake of an agreed decision, and on the assumption that other participants were doing the same, they took the risk of having to accept a result they did not want. So the Dissenter cannot, now that the result turns out to be contrary to his own views, claim that he never accepted the validity of the decision-procedure and is therefore under no obligation to obey it. At the relevant time, his behaviour was such as to lead people reasonably to believe that he did accept the decision-procedure.

I should say a little more to justify my claim that it was reasonable to assume, from the Dissenter's behaviour, that he accepted the validity of the decision-procedure. It must, I think, be reasonable to assume consent on the part of a person who votes without in any way indicating that his vote is not to be taken as an indication of consent. This must be reasonable, not because people who vote as a matter of fact usually do consent, but because there is a conceptual connection between voting and consenting. What would be the sense of having a vote if no one ever accepted the result of the vote? If this were the case, voting would be as pointless as promising would be if people were no more likely to do what they promised to do than what they merely said they might do. Of course, this does not mean that everyone who votes actually consents to this method of settling disputes, any more than the conceptual connection between promising and doing what one promised means that everyone actually keeps his promises. It only means that the normal case of voting must, because of what voting is, be a case in which there is consent. This, however, is enough to establish the point I want to make, that it is reasonable to assume that someone does consent if he votes, voluntarily and without indicating that he does not consent.[1]

It is interesting that there is, in law, a notion which closely parallels what I have said about quasi-consent.[2] This is the notion of estoppel. The essentials of one important form of estoppel, estoppel by representation, as stated by Lord Birkenhead in a leading case, are:

Where A has by his words or conduct justified B in believing that a certain state of affairs exists, and B has acted upon such belief to his prejudice, A is not permitted to affirm against B that a different state of facts existed at the same time.[3]

The effect of this doctrine is to prevent someone denying something which, by his voluntary behaviour, he led another reasonably to believe. In estoppel, as in what I have called quasi-consent, the real intention is irrelevant:

[1] F. Siegler, in 'Plamenatz on Consent and Obligation', *Philosophical Quarterly*, vol. 18 (1968), p. 261, acknowledges that there is an entailment between the existence of free elections and general consent by the voters to the authority of the system, but says '. . . of course, this metaphysical-sounding truth is not even close to a justification for political obligation.' I hope I have shown that this truth, while it may not justify a consensual obligation does play an important part in justifying a quasi-consensual obligation. See also J. Jenkins, 'Political Consent', *Philosophical Quarterly*, vol. 20 (1970), pp. 60–6.

[2] This parallel was pointed out to me by John Dwyer.

[3] *Maclaine* v. *Gatty* [1921] 1.A.C. 376, at p. 386, H.L. Quoted in Spencer, Bower, and Turner, *The Law Relating to Estoppel by Misrepresentation* (Butterworths, London, 2nd ed., 1966), p. 4.

If, whatever a man's real intention may be, he so conducts himself that a reasonable man would take the representation to be true . . . the party making the representation will be equally precluded from contesting its truth.[1]

The legal doctrine of estoppel, then, serves as a useful illustration of what I am saying about voting. In voting, one's voluntary behaviour leads others to the reasonable belief that one consents to the majority decision-procedure. After the event, one cannot say that one never consented—or to be strictly accurate, even if one says that one never consented, one is still obliged as if one had consented. Even if a person never consented, and never intended that his action should be taken as indicative of consent, so long as he knew that the purpose of the election was to reach an agreed decision, that is enough. We might say, if we were lawyers, that under these circumstances, you are estopped from denying that you consented.

This account of the obligation of the voter to obey the outcome of the process in which he participates is not open to the usual objections made against consent theories of obligation in a democracy. It is sometimes said that by voting in an election a person actually consents to be bound by the results of the election, but this view has been forcefully rejected on the grounds that it is absurd to say that a person who votes *against* the successful candidate consents to his election.[2] To this objection it is possible to reply, on grounds similar to those on which I have based my argument about the normal case of voting, that since the purpose of an election is to select one of the candidates for a position of authority, a voter who, knowing this, freely takes part in the election does

[1] Parke, B. in *Freeman* v. *Cooke* [1848] 2 Exch. 654, at p. 663. Quoted in Spencer, Bower, and Turner, op. cit., p. 90.

[2] See A. D. Lindsay, *Essentials of Democracy* (Clarendon Press, Oxford, 1929), pp. 14–15; T. McPherson, *Political Obligation* (Routledge, London, 1967), pp. 21–2.

consent to the conferring of that authority on the person who receives most votes, even if that should happen to be a candidate against whom he voted.[1] This reply, however, is not totally convincing. People sometimes vote without accepting the legitimacy of the electoral procedure, simply because they can see nothing better to do. Lenin, for instance, regarded capitalist democracy as a mere cloak for capitalist rule, but he urged Communists to 'utilize reactionary parliaments in a truly revolutionary way', so as to hasten revolution. Even someone less extreme than Lenin, faced, say, with the kind of choice citizens of the United States had in the 1968 Presidential elections, might have voted for Humphrey as the lesser evil, without consenting to the electoral system which presented him with the alternatives of Nixon and Humphrey, and thus without consenting to the election of either candidate.[2] If we make it quite clear, however, that the obligation arising from participation does not depend on actual consent at all, but merely on the act of participation, then we are not open to objections based on the fact that some voters reject the whole electoral system.

It is worth noting here that many people are aware (sometimes as a result of careful reasoning, perhaps more often intuitively) that participating in an election indicates support for the electoral system and gives rise to an obligation to accept its results. Before the Presidential election of 1968, for instance,

[1] J. P. Plamenatz, in the 1968 Postscript to the second edition of *Consent, Freedom and Political Obligation*, p. 170. See also the same author's *Man and Society* (Longmans, London, 1963), vol. 1, pp. 239–40. In the first edition of *Consent, Freedom and Political Obligation*, Plamenatz held views similar to those of Lindsay and McPherson.

[2] This objection has been made by F. Siegler, op. cit.; by K. Greenawalt, 'A Contextual Approach to Disobedience', *Nomos*, vol. 12 (1970), p. 334; and by M. Cohen, 'Liberalism and Disobedience', *Philosophy and Public Affairs*, vol. 1, (1972), pp. 311–12. Plamanatz has been defended by J. Jenkins, op. cit.

an organization known as Resist, representing a large number of groups opposed to the war in Vietnam and the draft, ran a campaign urging people not to vote in the forthcoming election. In full-page advertisements, they argued, in part, as follows:

In 1968 the electoral arena presents Americans with no pretence of a meaningful choice . . . There are hardly another two men in American public life whose commitment to the Cold War and to every step of the Southeast Asian escalation has been more un-swerving than that of Nixon and Humphrey . . . The resistance movement . . . refuses now to engage in a futile search for the lesser evil; and it will not participate in sanctioning evil by voting for any of the leading Presidential candidates in this election.[1]

This statement was signed by, among others, Noam Chomsky, Paul Goodman, Bishop James Pike, and Benjamin Spock. At the same time, the Youth International Party (Yippies) and their allies were holding marches and planning to picket polling places in order to support their claim that 'a vote for any of the main candidates constitutes tacit approval of a system that ignores the views of the people'. (Jerry Rubin was reported to have urged people to demonstrate their feelings about the election by undressing in polling booths.)[2] My argument is an attempt to show why these people, feeling as they did that they should not put themselves under an obligation to obey either Nixon or Humphrey, were right to refuse to vote.

Someone might say the Yippies and the members of Resist could, like my hypothetical beer drinker, have announced before voting that they rejected the system in which they were about to participate and would not necessarily abide by the result. In this way they would have increased the chances of a Humphrey victory (assuming that Humphrey was the lesser evil) without incurring any obligation to either Humphrey or

[1] From an advertisement in the *New York Review of Books*, 10 Oct. 1968.
[2] *The Times*, 1 Nov. 1968.

Nixon. To consider this point, let us return to our simplified model of a democratic society.

What difference will it make to his obligations if the Dissenter announces to the meeting, before the vote on *The News*, that his participation in the vote should not be taken as an indication that, if the vote goes against him, he will accept and obey that decision? This suggestion may strike us as improbable, but it does seem that the Dissenter will then not have the same obligation to obey the majority decision as he would have if he had not made the announcement. On the other hand, other members might ask themselves why they should not make similar announcements; but if they did, there would cease to be any point in voting on the issue, since the majority verdict would not be accepted, and hence would decide nothing. We have here a schematic representation of the breakdown of a democratic system. Whether or not the Dissenter's act will in fact lead to the breakdown of democracy, the Dissenter is clearly taking an unfair position, a position which allows him to have a say in the decision, and yet not be obliged by any decision opposed to his views. This position is made possible only by the restraint of others, who could benefit by doing as the Dissenter does, and think they have as good reason to do so as he has, but accept the obligations of the democratic process because of a desire to preserve it.

To vote, and yet refuse to be in any way obliged by the result of the vote, is to take an advantage over those who are prepared to accept the majority decision. It is unfair because it violates a rule essential to democracy. The Dissenter's reason for taking his special position depends on his claim that he is right. But others believe just as sincerely that they are right. The existence of democracy depends on them subordinating their desire to act on this belief to their support for the democratic decision-procedure.

There would be, for this reason, a strong case for barring

from participation in the democratic process those who announce beforehand that they do not regard the result of the election as obliging them to the smallest degree, or that they consider the process fraudulent, or that the majority has no right to decide the matter on which they are voting. In practice, of course, this would be a difficult test to apply, and it might also be inexpedient for another reason—it would afford the dissenters a marvellous opportunity for propaganda against the 'tyranny' that deprived them of the most elementary democratic right of voting. This deprivation would not really be tyrannous, indeed it would be in accordance with the theoretical principles of democracy, but it would be easy to make it appear tyrannous.

I should also note that what I have been saying applies in a relatively straightforward way if voting is voluntary, but becomes more complicated when voting is compulsory. In Australia, for example, one can be fined for failing to vote, and it would therefore seem that voting cannot give rise to any obligation, since it would not be reasonable to assume consent, even in normal cases, from a coerced act. On the other hand, it is still possible to spoil one's ballot paper, and so be counted as an informal voter. The difficulty is that voting is secret, so that no one can know whether one really has spoilt the ballot paper. One would have to announce that one has done so, and the announcement would have to be taken on trust. Alternatively, one could refuse to vote and pay the fine. I am doubtful, though, whether it would be necessary to resort to either of these alternatives, for it may be better to regard any degree of compulsion as negating the obligation that would otherwise arise. If so, this is a reason against compelling people to vote, although other factors are again relevant.[1]

[1] The importance of avoiding compulsion if voting is to generate any kind of consensual obligation has been pointed out by D. D. Raphael, *Problem of Political Philosophy* (Macmillan, London, 1971), pp. 112-13.

Once again, it is necessary to say a little more about the reason I am arguing for, if it is to appeal to utilitarians, who may not regard unfairness as bad in itself. It must be shown that this unfairness is likely to have undesirable consequences, and if this reason, arising from participation, is to be separate from and additional to the 'fair compromise' argument advanced earlier, it must be shown why participation makes any difference to the consequences of disobedience. I think it does make a difference in two ways. First, while public obedience will support, and public disobedience weaken, the decision-procedure whether one has participated in it or not, participation, if known to others, is likely to intensify the effects of obeying or disobeying. Consider this analogy: in a particular industry there is a system of voluntary arbitration which is normally used to settle disputes between the unions and employers. If a union decides that it will not submit its case for a higher wage to the arbitration system on one occasion, this will weaken the system to some extent, and if it were to happen often enough, the system would become redundant. Consider, however, what would happen if the union were to go to arbitration (in circumstances in which the employers were perpared to accept whatever verdict the arbitrator reached) but then, on hearing the verdict, the union were to declare it to be unacceptable, and take other measures to gain a higher wage. It would, I believe, require far fewer occurrences of the second type to destroy the arbitration system than of the first. I believe also, although I have no way of proving it, that the same is true in respect of political institutions. This conclusion probably would not apply to secret disobedience, like the performance of illegal abortions, but it clearly would apply to any person or group who publicly urged people to vote in a certain way at an election, and then publicly urged them to disobey the result of that election.

The second way in which public participation makes a

difference is that it arouses expectations in others that one will accept the result of the process one has participated in. As we have seen, this is a reasonable expectation, since without general acceptance of the result of the process by those participating, the process would soon be abandoned. It is obvious that a refusal to accept the decision by those participating will disappoint these expectations in others, and will cause resentment and anger among those who did participate in good faith, ready to accept results to which they were opposed. These people have been taken advantage of; they have been treated as dumb, honest suckers by people who seemed to be acting in good faith, but were really only using the system for what they could get out of it. This, if not a wholly accurate picture, is how many of those who participated in good faith will see the matter, and the fact that the participants disobey publicly will seem to sincere voters to be a brazen flaunting of contempt for democratic procedures. This resentment is a utilitarian reason for accepting the verdict of a decision in which one has participated.

Obviously, if participation is a reason for obeying, it is one which does not apply to associations organized along the lines of the first and second models, in which the necessary participation is lacking. I should perhaps reiterate that even if from the point of view of democratic theory those who participate in a procedure must accept its results (and even here some qualifications have to be made, as we shall see) from the broader standpoint of morality in general, this is only one factor to be taken into account in deciding how to act. My claim is only that it is a significant consideration which should never be ignored. It may sometimes be overridden. In practical terms, this means that it may sometimes be wrong to disobey a law which has arisen from a decision-procedure in which one has voluntarily participated, in circumstances in which one would be justified in disobeying the same law if one had not participated in the system. This is a reason for obedience which is much more likely to apply in democratic societies than under other forms of government.

SUMMARY

Our discussion so far has been confined to model associations. By comparing three models, two of which were plainly undemocratic in their method of government, while the third was a model democratic association, I have examined the popular belief that while disobedience may be justifiable in an undemocratic society, there are special reasons for obeying the law in a democracy. Although some of the traditional grounds for this belief have proved unsatisfactory, I believe I have shown that there are at least two significant reasons for obeying the law in a model democracy which do not apply to other political systems. To this extent the popular belief has been confirmed.

I have said nothing up to now about the relation between the two reasons for obedience for which I have argued. I said, firstly, that one ought to accept a decision-procedure which represented a fair compromise between competing claims to power. 'Accept' here involves both participating in and abiding by the results of the decision-procedure. Secondly, I argued that participation in a decision-procedure, when others are participating in good faith, creates a *prima facie* obligation to accept the results of the procedure. Taking these two points in conjunction, we can see that the first is particularly important because it provides a reason for participating in the democratic process as well as for accepting its verdict. Without this reason for participating, the second reason would lack grip, in that understanding the obligation involved in participating might lead one to refuse to participate.

Obviously, I have not discussed all the possible reasons for obeying the law which are specially relevant to democracies. I have discussed what seem to me to be the main ones, but there are many others. Since obeying the laws of any political system is one way of supporting that system, and any reason one has for favouring a political system is also a reason for supporting it, any feature of a political system of which one approves is a reason for obeying the laws of that system. When comparing democratic and undemocratic political systems, any advantages that the former have over the latter may be regarded as reasons for obeying democratic laws which do not apply to non-democratic systems. So any argument for democracy, for instance, J. S. Mill's claim that the active role played by members of a democratic society enhances their dignity and even their intellectual capacities[1] is, if valid, a specifically democratic reason for obedience. To discuss all the specifically democratic reasons for obedience would therefore involve discussing all the possible reasons for preferring democracy to other systems of government. To come to a balanced conclusion one would have to offset all these reasons against whatever reasons there are for preferring non-democratic forms of government. Rather than undertake a sketchy resumé of reasons of this sort (only a few of which can be settled without a very careful study of controversial matters of fact) I will refer the reader to the literature which exists on the subject.[2] Instead, in the following pages I shall go on to what seem to me to be the two main tasks needed to follow up what I have said so far. Firstly, I shall discuss some objections, and

---

[1] J. S. Mill, *Representative Government*, esp. pp. 203-4.

[2] This literature is extensive, going back at least to Plato's *Republic* including such nineteenth-century classics as Mill's *Representative Government*, and works of this century as different as A. D. Lindsay's *Essentials of Democracy* (Clarendon Press, Oxford, 1929) and R. A. Dahl's *Preface to Democratic Theory* (University of Chicago Press, Chicago, 1956).

make some qualifications to the conclusions reached so far. Then I shall consider the extent to which these conclusions, reached by a consideration of model associations, are applicable to the forms of government in those countries which we in the West think of as democracies.

PART II

OBJECTIONS AND QUALIFICATIONS

PEOPLE disobey the law for a variety of moral reasons, and the form their disobedience takes varies considerably. These different aims and forms make a difference to the justification of disobedience, and to the extent to which the specifically democratic reasons for obedience apply.

In considering these factors, we shall often have to try to take account of relevant matters of fact about particular societies. This is unavoidable if we are to discuss the actual justifications of disobedience put forward by its practitioners. Since disobedience always takes place in a particular context, the arguments used to defend it are not abstract; they rely on various facts about the society in which the disobedience takes place. To ignore these facts would be to give up the claim that our arguments are relevant to those who participate, or think about participating, in acts of disobedience.

Our concern in this part of the book is with those arguments in defence of disobedience which deny or overlook the reasons for obedience which I have argued are relevant to democratic societies (though I remind the reader that we have yet to consider whether any existing systems of government conform sufficiently to the democratic model for the democratic reasons to hold). I have no theoretical disagreements with those who recognize the reasons for obedience in a democracy, but consider that very special, weighty considerations—for example, the prolonged horror of the war in Vietnam—outweigh these democratic obligations. Whether, in a particular case, the democratic obligations are outweighed is not something which can be determined in the abstract, and to expect any work of theory to give answers to such questions is to expect more than theory alone can give.

RIGHTS AGAINST THE MAJORITY

There is a tradition in democratic thought which links democracy with a theory of rights. Majority rule, according to this tradition, is only a part of democracy, or at least, of 'constitutional democracy', which is the only kind of democracy worth the name. Just as essential to democracy are limits on the scope of majority action, limits which leave to the individual inviolable freedoms, beyond the legitimate reach of the majority. The classic statement of this view is the American Declaration of Independence:

We hold these truths to be self-evident: that all men are created equal; that they are endowed by their Creator with certain inalienable rights; that among these are life, liberty and the pursuit of happiness; that to secure these rights, governments are instituted among men, deriving their just powers from the consent of the governed; that whenever any form of government becomes destructive of these ends it is the right of the people to alter or to abolish it . . .

It is hardly surprising that the belief that democracy involves respect for rights should be most widely held in the United States, but it can also be found almost everywhere democratic ideas are to be found. A powerful defence of disobedience can be based on it. If men have inviolable rights, that is, rights which ought never to be violated, any decision which denies these rights can have no moral claim to be obeyed. So the reasons for obedience for which I have argued must be treated as having limits which make them inapplicable when the majority decision interferes with rights.

In order to discuss this line of thought, it will be convenient to deal separately with two classes of rights: those that are essential for the preservation of a system of government sufficiently like that of our third model association to give rise to the reasons for obedience for which I have argued, and those which are not essential for this. I will first consider rights in the former group, and to facilitate discussion I will revert to the third model association.

Imagine that in the third association there is a majority of members who strongly dislike certain views held by a few members on how the association should be run. Naturally, the few cannot put their views into effect, since they are a minority, but they hope that they will eventually convert a majority of members to their views. In order to prevent this, the majority pass a motion that no one should be allowed to speak in support of these views. What reaction to this decision would be in accordance with the aspects of the decision-procedure of the third model association which give rise to the special reasons for obeying it? (For convenience, I shall refer to these aspects as 'democratic principles'.)

A selective restriction of the right to free speech is contrary to democratic principles. By a selective restriction, I mean one which picks out certain views, and says that no one may speak or write in favour of these views, although other views are not proscribed; alternatively, a selective restriction might prevent some people from supporting any political views at all, while allowing others to support whatever views they like. In either case, the restriction destroys the fair compromise which is the basis of democratic obligations, since it favours some members of the society over others—some have the means of winning other members over to their views, others do not.

A restriction of the right to free speech which was not selective but total would appear not to favour any particular members of the society over others. It is difficult, however, to imagine such a proposal being made seriously, outside a Trappist monastery. Even the most totalitarian states bombard their citizens with the views of the ruling clique. In a democracy, free speech has obvious advantages in promoting informed decision-making, which is more likely to be right than uninformed decision-making. Nevertheless, the idea of a total ban is of theoretical interest, because it suggests that not every ban on free speech will be undemocratic. If people wished to avoid debating issues almost as much as they wished to avoid fighting over them, they might accept as a fair compromise a system in which issues were decided by a vote, but no one was allowed to speak for or against any proposal. More realistically, a democratic society may adopt procedural rules which limit the amount of debate on any issue, or the amount of canvassing that any candidate for office may do. These rules are all restrictions on free speech, but they are restrictions which apply equally to everyone, no matter who he is and what views he supports. Unlike selective restrictions, they do not violate the principle of fair compromise, and so do not affect this democratic reason for obedience. Selective restrictions do vitiate this reason for obedience. Where there are selective restrictions on free speech, those considering whether to disobey do not have to take into account this specifically democratic reason for obedience.

It is perhaps anomalous that the argument just advanced applies in a more straightforward way to any decisions reached by the association while the decision restricting freedom of speech is operative, than to the original motion itself, since this motion was passed under conditions of free speech, and therefore under a fair decision-procedure. It seems to follow that the fairness of the decision-procedure up to and including this decision is a reason for accepting and participating in it, and that this participation gives rise to a further reason for obedience, in the normal way. It is only to later decisions that these reasons for obedience no longer apply. With regard to the particular decision restricting free speech, we seem to be forced to say that while there are democratic reasons for disobeying (to restore the fair compromise) there are also democratic reasons for obeying. If there is a clash here, all one can say is that both factors must be taken into account. Perhaps they cancel each other out, or perhaps, as I am inclined to think, freedom of speech is such a fundamental requirement that any reasonable chance of restoring it outweighs the reasons for obedience. In any case, I do not think that this clash indicates any serious inconsistency in democratic principles. The same kind of conflict of reasons may be found in very simple political doctrines. If an absolute monarch were to make an irrevocable grant of all his powers to an elected assembly, the absolutist principle that one ought to obey only the hereditary monarch could be cited both for and against obedience to the decision. This problem can arise in respect of any sovereign decision-procedure, because sovereignty involves the power to modify or change altogether the decision-procedure in operation. If it be decided by decision-procedure X that decision-procedure Y should be instituted, this will always lead to a dilemma for someone who has championed X against Y.

What is true of the right to freedom of speech is also true, for the same reasons, of any other right essential to the operation of a decision-procedure like that of the third association. Among these are the right to vote or stand for office, or the right to freedom of association and peaceful assembly, and so on. More complete lists of the rights essential to democracy can be found in any standard text on the subject.[1] As there is some controversy over the details, I will avoid giving a complete list. Some further discussion of what is to count as a fair

[1] One such list can be found in R.A. Dahl, *Polyarchy* (Yale U.P., New Haven and London, 1971), p. 3.

democratic system will be found below, in Part III. In general, then, the very nature of the democratic process involves the existence of rights, the violation of which invalidates the reasons for obedience to which the democratic process normally gives rise. Strictly speaking, the violation will (unless it is a violation of the right to vote) invalidate only the reason for obedience derived from fair compromise, and not that derived from voluntary participation; but if the fair compromise has ceased to operate, there will be little point in participating.

If the question be put: who is to decide when a right essential to democracy has been violated? the answer can only be: the individual. As we saw in considering the problem of minorities, the decision as to the fairness of the decision-procedure cannot be left to the decision-procedure itself. The only other possible solution, that of setting up some body independent of the decision-procedure, is not, in practice, a real possibility. Ultimately such bodies must be under the control of the decision-procedure, for someone must appoint the members of the body. The Supreme Court of the United States, for instance, has never really been an effective guardian of minority rights against the majority—it has generally followed public thinking after a decent interval.[1]

When we turn to rights which are not essential to a system of government sufficiently like that of our third model to give rise to the special reasons for obedience, the situation is different. Among the rights of this sort which people have demanded are the right of freedom of worship, the right to attend the same schools as people of other races, the right to equal pay, and the right to have sexual intercourse with persons of one's own sex. (The violation of some of these rights might,

[1] See R. A. Dahl, *Pluralist Democracy in the United States: Conflict and Consent* (Rand McNally, Chicago, 1967), ch. 6.

of course, be part of a policy of discrimination against a minority which would, as explained earlier, be incompatible with fair compromise.) The right to life can be construed either broadly or narrowly, so that it may or may not be essential to democratic government. Broadly construed, the right to life would prohibit capital punishment under any circumstances. A violation of this right, say in cases of murder, would not be contrary to democratic principles. On a more narrow construction of the right to life, only some arbitrary taking of life would count as a breach. Needless to say, some arbitrary killing would destroy the basis of democracy—the killing of those who held certain views must be at least as contrary to democratic principles as the banning of those views! So just when a right is essential to democracy and when not will require judgement. Once we have decided that a right is not essential to democracy, however, it is clear that the violation of such rights does not destroy the basis of the democratic reasons for obedience. Again, I emphasize that the violation of non-essential rights may be so serious as to justify disobedience despite the democratic reasons for obedience; my point is only that in this case the disobedience is 'despite' these reasons. When the rights violated are essential to democracy, there is no need for the democratic reasons to be over-ridden, and so a less serious violation may justify disobedience.

There is a further complication to what I have just said, because whether we regard a violation of a particular right as 'undemocratic' will depend on our concept of democracy. Since the term 'democratic' has favourable connotations, many government actions are called 'undemocratic' by their opponents, even though the actions in no way interfere with the decision-procedure. There is nothing really wrong with a broad concept of 'democracy', although I think it helps clear thinking to restrict the term's meaning. If one does regard rights which are not essential to a decision-procedure like that of the third model association as none the less democratic rights, then one could hold that democratic principles (here the phrase means more than the principles of the third model decision-procedure) support disobedience against any violation of these rights by the majority. What one may not hold, I contend, is that the democratic reasons for obedience generated by the decision-procedure of the third model do not hold in such a case. So long as the violations of rights do not undermine the decision-procedure, these reasons must be taken into account.

The difference between a broad and a narrow concept of democracy, so far as the present discussion is concerned, amounts only to this: when a decision made by a decision-procedure like that of the third model violates an important, but non-essential right, say, the right to freedom of worship, I, with my narrower concept of democracy, would say that this creates a clash between the special democratic reasons for obeying (as well as any other reasons for obeying there might be) and the reason for disobeying, which is the injustice, hardship, or violation of rights, caused by the decision. We have to decide which of these reasons are more important. Someone with a broader concept of democracy, who regarded freedom of worship as an essential democratic right, would say that in the situation described, there was a clash between democratic principles, some of which favour obedience, and some disobedience. Provided we are clear about what we mean by 'democratic', so that holding the broader concept does not lead us to think that we can ignore the force of what I call the democratic reasons for obedience, the difference seems to be merely verbal.

The substantial issue, then, is that the difference between rights essential to, and rights not essential to the functioning of a decision-procedure like that of the third association must be recognized. It does not matter if this difference is held to lie within, or outside 'democracy'. The difference is important because, as I have already said, when a decision is made which gives one reason to believe that the decision-procedure is not, or can no longer, operate as a fair compromise, there is no point in appealing to the decision-procedure itself to determine whether this is so. Hence there is no real alternative to allowing those concerned to decide for themselves. With suspected violations of rights which are not essential to the fair operation of the decision-procedure, however, it is possible to leave it to the decision-procedure to resolve what rights are to be respected. On practical grounds, there is good reason to do so. A vast amount of the normal legislation of a modern government can be seen as a violation of some right or other. Segregated schools are to most of us a clear violation of a right to equal treatment, but to some people legislation against segregated schools is a violation of a right to send one's children to whatever school one wants, or an infringement of the right of the local community to govern itself on these matters. (I think it is partly because segregation, as practised in the American South, was a clear indication of unfairness towards a minority, and thus violated the democratic reasons for obedience, while the right to send one's children to whatever school one wants is not essential to the democratic procedure, that civil disobedience against segregation was justified, but the disobedience of segregationists against federal integration orders was not.) Minimum wage legislation has been seen as contrary to the right of freedom of contract; fluoridation as a violation of a right to refuse medicine; some people think that legal abortion disregards the rights of the unborn, while others demand abortion as a woman's right to control her own body; even taxation can be said to infringe the right to property. The list is endless. If a democratic decision-procedure is to perform its function of resolving disputes peacefully, the individual must recognize that there are strong reasons for allowing a fair decision-procedure to determine which of these alleged rights are really to be treated as rights.[1]

So my conclusion is that the reasons for obedience which hold in democratic societies are not limited by any theories of rights, except when the rights infringed are essential for the continued existence of the decision-procedure in the form which gave rise to the reasons for obedience.

DISOBEDIENCE FOR PUBLICITY

The example of an act of disobedience which I discussed in connection with the simplified models was an act intended to prevent, physically, the carrying out of the decision of the association. In discussing this example I have written as if disobedience is always like this, always an attempt to force the alteration of a decision, or make it impossible for the decision to be effective. I must now acknowledge that disobedience can take other forms. The rest of this part of the book will be concerned with forms of disobedience which do not involve coercion. My aim will be to assess the difference the form disobedience takes has on the democratic reasons for obedience.

I shall begin by quoting from an article written by Bertrand Russell in support of the campaign of civil disobedience organized by the 'Committee of 100' against British nuclear policies. I quote at some length because Russell's is an

---

[1] These remarks are relevant to R. Dworkin's article 'Taking Rights Seriously', *New York Review of Books*, 17 Dec. 1970. Probably the fundamental difference between my position and Dworkin's is over the nature of rights, an issue that I cannot discuss properly here. What I can say is that even on Dworkin's view of rights, while a person may always have a right to disobey when the state infringes a right of his, to say this leaves untouched the question of whether he ought to exercise that right. So if one accepted a theory of rights like that of Dworkin, I would still argue that the democratic reasons for obedience count against exercising the right to disobey.

articulate defence of disobedience in a country generally regarded as democratic. More recent defences of disobedience have not always been as carefully reasoned.

Those who study nuclear weapons and the probable course of nuclear war are divided into two classes. There are, on the one hand, people employed by governments, and on the other hand, unofficial people who are actuated by a realization of the dangers and catastrophes which are probable if governmental policies remain unchanged. There are a number of questions in dispute. I will mention a few of them. What is the likelihood of a nuclear war by accident? What is to be feared from fall-out? What proportion of the population is likely to survive an all-out nuclear war? On every one of these questions independent students find that official apologists and policy-makers give answers which, to the unbiased inquirer, appear grossly and murderously misleading. To make known to the general population what independent inquirers believe to be the true answers to these questions is a very difficult matter. Where the truth is difficult to ascertain there is a natural inclination to trust the official authorities. This is especially the case when what they assert enables people to dismiss uneasiness as needlessly alarmist. The major organs of publicity feel themselves part of the Establishment and are very reluctant to take a course which the Establishment will frown on. Long and frustrating experience has proved, to those among us who have endeavoured to make unpleasant facts known, that orthodox methods, alone, are insufficient. By means of civil disobedience, a certain kind of publicity becomes possible. What we do is reported, though as far as possible our reasons for what we do are not mentioned. The policy of suppressing our reasons, however, has only very partial success. Many people are roused to inquire into questions which they had been willing to ignore. Many people, especially among the young, come to share the opinion that governments, by means of lies and evasions, are luring whole populations to destruction. It seems not unlikely that, in the end, an irresistible popular movement of protest will compel governments to allow their subjects to continue to exist. On the basis of long experience, we are convinced that this object cannot be achieved by law-abiding methods alone. Speaking for myself, I regard this as the most important reason for adopting civil disobedience.[1]

For the purposes of discussion, I shall assume that the facts are as Russell states them to be in this passage.

The first point to notice is the importance of the issue. The issue in this case—nuclear policies and the possibility of nuclear war—is obviously sufficiently important to bring disobedience into consideration. Secondly, there is the point that the government has a great advantage in putting its case to the public, partly because the true facts are alarming and people prefer not to be alarmed, and partly because the major organs of publicity are biased in favour of the government. Russell's conclusion, confirmed by experience, is that orthodox methods are insufficient to gain the dissenters a reasonable hearing for their views. Civil disobedience, Russell claims, is therefore justified because it will help to gain a fair hearing, otherwise denied, to a dissenting group on a matter of supreme importance. The final goal is a popular movement which will lead to a change in government policies. It is not entirely clear whether this movement is expected to work by constitutional methods, once a fair hearing has been obtained by disobedience, but to simplify discussion we shall assume that this is the case.

The kind of disobedience for which Russell argues, then, is not an attempt by a minority to coerce a majority. It is a means of presenting a case to a majority, an attempt to persuade rather than to coerce. Russell is, in effect, appealing to some principle of fairness, claiming that the difficulties and distortions which his views have to overcome in reaching the voters through normal channels are so great as to destroy the

[1] 'Civil Disobedience and the Threat of Nuclear Warfare', first published in C. Urquhart (ed.), *A Matter of Life* (Cape, London, 1963), and reprinted in H. A. Bedau (ed.) *Civil Disobedience: Theory and Practice*, pp. 156–7.

basis of the normal democratic reasons for obedience. We have seen that fair compromise requires that there be no bias in the way in which differing views reach the members of the society. Russell's disobedience, far from denying the democratic reasons for obedience for which I have argued, can be seen as a way of remedying defects in a system which, in practice, has departed from the basic conditions on which democracy, and the democratic reasons for obedience, depend.

The principal difficulty in assessing this kind of argument is in deciding what constitutes a sufficiently unbiased hearing for differing views. One simple and superficially attractive answer is that formal freedom of expression is all that is needed. So long as no one is legally barred from expressing whatever political views he likes, the requirement of equality is satisfied. Russell, of course, would deny this. He points out that in a large society, 'the major organs of publicity' have much more influence than ordinary 'unofficial people'. Moreover, Russell says, these major organs of publicity are part of the Establishment, and so predisposed towards Establishment views.

Russell is surely right to claim that formal freedom is not enough in a society like ours. The proprietor of a major newspaper has a better opportunity of influencing government decisions, should he so desire, than the man on a soap-box at Speakers' Corner, even though legally they have the same freedom of expression. It might be said that equality is preserved because everyone has an equal opportunity to become the proprietor of a major newspaper, but this is untrue, because inherited wealth, or better still inherited newspaper holdings, certainly make it easier. In any case, even if an ordinary worker could work himself up to be a newspaper proprietor, he would then no longer be an ordinary worker, so that the views of workers might still fail to find expression.

If formal freedom is not enough, what would constitute an adequate hearing? Unfortunately, Russell never spells this out.

There is a tendency for dissenters to take the fact that their view has not been accepted by the public as evidence that it has not been properly presented to the public. This is obviously a mistake, though one which is hard to avoid if one is convinced that one's own view is indisputably correct. Russell himself was not immune to this danger. Although it may be a little unkind to Russell, I will quote an instance which may serve to remind dissenters how easily one can fall into this mistake. In another leaflet, entitled 'On Civil Disobedience' Russell wrote:

. . . the forces that control opinion are heavily weighted upon the side of the rich and powerful . . . The ignorance of important public men on the subject of nuclear warfare is utterly astounding to those who have made an impartial study of the subject. And from public men this ignorance trickles down to become the voice of the people. It is against this massive artificial ignorance that our protests are directed. I will give a few instances of this astonishing ignorance: . . . the Prime Minister recently stated without any qualification that 'there will be no war by accident'. I have not come across one non-government expert who has studied this subject who does not say the opposite. C. P. Snow, who has an exceptional right to speak with authority, said in a recent article 'Within at the most ten years, some of these bombs are going off. I am saying this as responsibly as I can. *That* is a certainty.'[1]

Today, with the benefit of more than ten years' hindsight, we are not likely to feel so sure that the influence of the rich and powerful produced a 'massive artificial ignorance' which was responsible for the rejection of the views of Russell and Snow on the likelihood of an accidental nuclear war.

Can we say that if the mass media allow dissenters opportunities to put their own case, this will be sufficient to ensure a fair hearing? There are difficulties even with this idea. Firstly, what

[1] First published 1961, reprinted in *The Autobiography of Bertrand Russell*, vol. 3 (Allen and Unwin, London, 1969), pp. 141–2, emphasis in original.

views are to be included, and how much time or space are the proponents of these views to be given? To give equal time and space to every possible view might seem to be a 'fair compromise' but it would probably mean that no one had enough time or space to develop his views properly; nor is it obviously a fair compromise if views held by one person have as much coverage as those held by millions—indeed it would pay political parties, under such a system, to disband and present themselves as individuals each holding slightly different views. Yet once we abandon this simple equality, how can bias be avoided? If we wished to present, say, a coverage of views on the war in Vietnam, do we limit ourselves to representatives of those for and against assisting the Saigon Government, or do we include those who wish to assist the National Liberation Front? It seems impossible to produce any general principles which can answer this kind of question. Nevertheless, in actual situations it may be possible to say when a particular view has had a fair hearing and when it has not. In the case of the American debate on the war in Vietnam, for instance, it would be reasonable to say that opposition to the war did not, at first, get a fair hearing. In the early sixties, the mass media tended to brand opposition as 'communist-inspired' or 'unpatriotic', and the government seriously misled the public about the nature and extent of American involvement. It was, I think, reasonable to claim at that time that disobedience was needed in order to put the case against the war to the American public. By the early seventies, however, the situation had changed, and disobedience for publicity purposes could not be considered necessary. For whatever reasons (quite possibly because of earlier campaigns of disobedience) the case against the war has been very fully presented by the media, and informative government documents on the war have been published (though mostly without government permission). The fact that the case against the war has now been adequately presented does not, however, mean that the case in favour of continuing American assistance to the Saigon Government has not received adequate coverage. That would be an unreasonable claim, in the face of the wide coverage that has been given to the views of the Nixon administration. The American coverage of the Vietnam issue in the early seventies suggests, therefore, that adequate presentation of opposed views is possible.

A deeper objection to the possibility of a satisfactory presentation of radical views on the mass media has been made by Herbert Marcuse, who believes that tolerance itself can be repressive. According to Marcuse:

> . . . within a repressive society, even progressive movements threaten to turn into their opposite to the degree to which they accept the rules of the game. To take a most controversial case: the exercise of political rights (such as voting, letter-writing to the press, to Senators, etc., protest-demonstrations with *a priori* renunciation of counterviolence) in a society of total administration serves to strengthen this administration by testifying to the existence of democratic liberties which, in reality, have changed their content and lost their effectiveness. In such a case, freedom (of opinion, of assembly, of speech) becomes an instrument for absolving servitude.[1]

The core of Marcuse's argument is that while liberal views of tolerance were 'based on the proposition that men were (potential) individuals who could learn to hear and see and feel by themselves, to develop their own thoughts, to grasp their true interests and rights and capabilities . . .', people in modern capitalist societies are 'manipulated and indoctrinated individuals who parrot, as their own, the opinion of their masters. . .'[2] Hence, Marcuse thinks, the rationale of tolerance no longer prevails.

Marcuse may well be right in his criticisms of the traditional

[1] 'Repressive Tolerance' in R. P. Wolff, B. Moore, and H. Marcuse, *A Critique of Pure Tolerance* (Beacon Press, Boston, 1969), pp. 83–4.

[2] Ibid., p. 90.

liberal view of tolerance, the view epitomized in Mill's *On Liberty*. It is by no means as clear as Mill thought it was that unrestricted tolerance is the surest road to truth. We should be prepared to face the possibility that Mill's optimistic liberal argument fails. We must then ask whether, in agreeing with Marcuse that tolerance may fail to lead individuals to a true appreciation of their interests, rights, and capabilities, we are committed to agreeing that tolerance ought to be restricted; that as Marcuse suggests, toleration of speech and assembly should be withdrawn from 'groups and movements which promote aggressive policies, armament, chauvinism, discrimination on the grounds of race and religion, or which oppose the extension of public services, social security, medical care, etc.'[1]

I think that Marcuse is in error when he assumes that a rejection of the liberal belief that tolerance leads to truth implies a rejection of tolerance itself. This seems a straightforward step for Marcuse because he accepts the liberal idea that the aim of tolerance is truth. This idea is, I think, a mistake, one that parallels the belief that, because the opinion of the majority is no more likely to be right than the opinion of the minority, there can be no justification for a democratic system of government. Just as in this case it seemed to me that the justification of a democratic decision-procedure depended not on its prospects of being right more often than any other procedure, but on its advantages as a basis for a fair, peaceful means of settling disputes, so now I would argue that tolerance is to be justified not as a means of reaching the truth, but as a necessary concomitant of a peaceful decision-procedure, and also as a form of compromise in itself—that is, as a way of avoiding disputes over which views should be allowed free expression, and which banned.

Once again, this may seem a miserable, abject justification

[1] Ibid., p. 100.

for something as important as tolerance. 'What?' (I imagine the reader saying to himself) 'Does he think *nothing* worth fighting for?' If 'fighting' here means literally fighting to the death, then I do think almost any reasonable compromise that substitutes some less deadly form of contest is preferable. Moreover, even if I do not think that toleration is always the surest road to truth, I think that the views I regard as true (and many of these Marcuse would also accept) have a better chance of prevailing under conditions of tolerance than they would if tolerance were abandoned. For if tolerance were withdrawn, there is no reason to believe it would be withdrawn from just those groups which I, or Marcuse, oppose. On the contrary, men on the Right think tolerance should be withdrawn from groups I and Marcuse favour. The only way Marcuse could get his particular version of restricted tolerance into effect would be by a resort to force; and in this kind of contest, the Right have the odds stacked much more clearly in their favour than in the contest of persuasion under conditions of tolerance. Tolerance may be no sure road to truth, but truth is still less likely to emerge from a resort to force.

Let us return, then, to Russell's defence of disobedience as a means of obtaining a fair hearing. We have seen that although it is possible for dissenting views to obtain an adequate hearing even when the media are in the hands of a few private concerns (as in the case of the American coverage of anti-war views in the early seventies) there is also a danger that dissenting views will be denied such a hearing (as in the case of the same views a few years earlier). Unfortunately there seems to be no general principle which would enable us to decide when views are getting an adequate hearing; again, this must be left to judgement in each case. Assuming, though, that Russell was correct in claiming that the case against nuclear weapons had not received a fair hearing, the argument put forward against disobedience to a decision-procedure which represents a fair compromise would not apply to the kind of disobedience defended by Russell. Russell clearly does not advocate disobedience as a means of coercing the majority, and he does not withdraw from the idea of a fair compromise as a means of deciding issues—indeed, as we have just seen, he can appeal to this idea in support of his actions.

It might be thought, however, that the following argument can be brought against the use of disobedience as a means of presenting a case. If such disobedience really is an effective form of publicity, anyone with a cause which he feels is not being given adequate consideration by the public may use disobedience as a form of publicity. Others, in order to secure an equally effective presentation of their case, will have equally good grounds for resorting to disobedience. Presumably, if disobedience becomes widely used in this way, the novelty of this form of protest will disappear and both the media and the public will pay less attention to it. In order to achieve the same effect as was previously obtained by simple, non-violent disobedience, the scale and nature of disobedience will have to be escalated. There will come a time when non-violent disobedience receives little publicity, but violent disobedience, if on a sufficiently grand scale, can never really be ignored, and so will always be publicized. (In the late sixties, this seemed to be happening in the United States, but the process would now appear to have abated.) In this way, even disobedience for the sake of publicity, it could be argued, carries within it the seeds of destruction of the democratic process. Just as with disobedience designed to coerce the majority, democratic principles must lead us to reject disobedience for publicity, for otherwise the decision-procedure may break down into a system in which issues are decided by the ability and willingness of the disputants to use force and violence.

This kind of argument fails because it is possible to draw

limits to the kind of disobedience compatible with fair compromise which will exclude those forms of disobedience for the sake of publicity which do threaten the continuance of the democratic process. Firstly, if the aim of disobedience is to present a case to the public, then only such disobedience as is necessary to present this case is justified. The democratic requirement of free and fair presentation of all views does not demand constant repetition of any one view. This severely restricts the amount of disobedience which can be justified on these grounds. (As I shall argue shortly, however, disobedience, in some form, may still be allowable in order to demonstrate sincerity or strength of feeling.)

Next, if disobedience for publicity purposes is to be compatible with fair compromise, it must be non-violent. It must be non-violent, not just for the tactical reason that violence is likely to hinder the task of persuasion, nor because violence in itself is wrong, but because to use violence is to obliterate the distinction between disobedience for the sake of publicity and disobedience designed to coerce or intimidate the majority. It does not matter that one may be clear in one's own mind that one is not intending to coerce the majority. From the point of view of the public, violence is intimidatory and coercive. The onus of making clear the persuasive and non-coercive nature of his disobedience must rest on the person disobeying. I think this onus can be discharged only by non-violent disobedience.

The same reasoning suggests that even non-violent disobedience which causes great inconvenience to the majority, or makes it very difficult for the decision of the majority to be implemented, should also be avoided. For even non-violent disobedience may be an attempt to coerce the majority. When protesters against conscription refuse to register for military service, and engage in a campaign of sending in false registration forms, their aim is to force the abandoning of the conscription programme. The object of recent campaigns of this sort in the United States and Australia has been, as the protesters have proclaimed, to 'fuck the system'— to make it impossible for the government officials concerned to do their work, and thus to cause the breakdown of the machinery of conscription. Disobedience of this sort, though non-violent, is an attempt to coerce and not to persuade. Should other major groups of the community employ similar means, the democratic decision-procedure would break down, almost as surely as if they had tried to settle issues by violence. (Consider, for instance, the possibility of similar campaigns by right-wing extremists designed to make welfare legislation unworkable.)

Next, when breaking laws for publicity purposes, there are strong reasons for submitting to apprehension and punishment. Acceptance of punishment indicates support for the principle of law, and for the authority of the decision-procedure, so far as is compatible with the need to break the law to present one's case to the public.[1] While it may be necessary to break the law for publicity, it will hardly ever, in a democratic society, be necessary to evade punishment, since acceptance of punishment is normally a useful means to further publicity, in that court statements are often widely reported.[2] Only if there were no right of public trial, and no possibility of using punishment for publicity purposes, or if punishments were made draconian in order to prevent dissenters from publicizing their views

[1] Martin Luther King has said: 'an individual who breaks a law that conscience tells him is unjust, and willingly accepts the penalty by staying in jail to arouse the conscience of the community over its injustice, is in reality expressing the very highest respect for law.' 'Letter from Birmingham City Jail', *Liberation* (June 1963), reprinted in Bedau, *Civil Disobedience*, pp. 78–9. Gandhi held similar views: see his autobiography, *The Story of My Experiments with Truth* (Beacon Press, Boston, 1957), p. 413.

[2] See Russell's account of the use he made of his trial and imprisonment, *Autobiography*, vol. 3 pp. 115–18.

illegally, would evasion of punishment perhaps be compatible with disobedience for the sake of publicity.

Finally, disobedience of this sort can only be an adjunct to a major propaganda campaign, designed to influence opinion by whatever legal channels there are. As was the case with the disobedience Russell was supporting in the passage quoted, such disobedience should only be resorted to after more orthodox means have been tried in vain. (As we saw in our discussion of the model associations, however, it would be unrealistic to demand that orthodox means be 'exhausted' since some orthodox means are never exhausted; instead orthodox means should be tried until it is obvious that they are not going to succeed, or until there is a real danger that the damage will be done before they succeed.) Unless the legal means of persuasion are used to the utmost, those who resort to disobedience can hardly claim that they are doing it only because they have been unable to obtain a fair hearing in any other way.

DISOBEDIENCE AS A PLEA FOR RECONSIDERATION

A form of disobedience related to that just discussed aims, not at presenting a view to the public, but at prodding the majority into reconsidering a decision it has taken. A majority may act, or fail to act, without realizing that there are truly significant issues at stake, or the majority may not have considered the interests of all parties, and its decision may cause suffering in a way that was not foreseen. Disobedience, and especially disobedience followed by acceptance of punishment, may make the majority realize that what is for it a matter of indifference is of great importance to others. Disobedience which aims to make the majority reconsider in this way is not an attempt to coerce them, and within limits broadly similar to those just discussed in connection with disobedience for publicity, it is compatible with acceptance of a fair compromise as a means of settling issues. Once it becomes apparent that the majority are not willing to reconsider, however, this sort of disobedience must be abandoned. One way of ascertaining whether the majority are willing to reconsider is to hold a referendum. This is one argument in favour of a provision in a democratic system for referenda to be held at the request of a minority group, as in Switzerland.

Disobedience of this sort—by a minority who feel very strongly about an issue, against a decision taken by a majority to whom the matter is of no great importance—can help to mitigate one of the stock weaknesses of democratic theory. It has long been recognized that there is a danger of injustice in democracy because the democratic system takes no account of the intensity with which views are held, so that a majority which does not care very much about an issue can out-vote a minority for which the issue is of vital concern. By civil disobedience the minority can demonstrate the intensity of its feelings to the majority. If the majority did in fact make its decision through short-sightedness, and not because the hardship to the minority is an unavoidable evil, justified by a far greater good on the whole, it will have the opportunity of altering its decision. Where there is reason to believe that the majority does not feel strongly about a matter, disobedience causing a certain amount of inconvenience can be justified in order to test the strength of feeling of the majority. If minor inconvenience will cause the majority to alter its decision, this indicates that the original decision was one of those in which a largely apathetic majority imposes its will on a deeply concerned minority. Since, in theory, weighting votes according to intensity of feeling would give rise to a still fairer compromise than is achieved by giving everyone an equal vote, to cause such inconvenience to the majority would be compatible with fair compromise. If the majority makes it clear, however, that it is prepared to put up with inconvenience, it must be assumed that it is not, after all, apathetic about the issue.

It is of course possible that a decision by a majority causing hardship to a minority results neither from oversight, nor from a regrettable necessity, but is part of a policy of deliberate exploitation of the minority by a majority which does not have equal concern for the welfare of all its citizens. This kind of situation has been discussed earlier.

This is an appropriate point at which to consider the theory of civil disobedience proposed by John Rawls in his much-discussed book, *A Theory of Justice*,[1] for Rawls's conception of the proper role of disobedience in a constitutional democracy has much in common with the kind of disobedience we have just been discussing. According to Rawls, civil disobedience is an act which 'addresses the sense of justice of the community and declares that in one's considered opinion the principles of social co-operation among free and equal men are not being respected'.[2] Civil disobedience is here regarded as a form of address, or an appeal. Accordingly Rawls comes to conclusions similar to those I have reached about the form which such disobedience should take. It should, he says, be non-violent and refrain from hurting or interfering with others because violence or interference tends to obscure the fact that what is being done is a form of address. While civil disobedience may 'warn and admonish, it is not itself a threat'. Similarly, to show sincerity and general fidelity to law, one should be completely open about what one is doing, willing to accept the legal consequences of one's act.

I am therefore in agreement with Rawls on the main point: limited disobedience, far from being incompatible with a

[1] Clarendon Press, Oxford, 1972. The theory of civil disobedience is to be found in ch. 6, mostly in sects. 55, 57, and 59.

[2] Ibid., p. 364.

genuinely democratic form of government, can have an important part to play as a justifiable form of protest. There are,
however, some features of Rawls's position which I cannot
accept. These features derive from the theory of justice which
is the core of the book. The reader may have noticed that the
sentence I quoted above contains a reference to 'the sense of
justice of the community' and to the 'principles of social co-
operation among free and equal men'. Rawls's justification of
civil disobedience depends heavily on the idea that a community
has a sense of justice which is a single sense of justice on which
all can agree, at least in practice if not in all theoretical details.
It is the violation of this accepted basis of society which
legitimates disobedience. To be fair to Rawls, it must be said
that he is not maintaining that men ever do or did get together
and agree on a sense of justice, and on the principles of social
co-operation. Rather the idea is that a basically just society will
have a sense of justice that corresponds to the principles that
free and equal men would have chosen, had they met together
to agree, under conditions designed to ensure impartiality, to
abide by the basic principles necessary for social co-operation.
It should also be said that Rawls does not maintain that every
society in fact has such a sense of justice, but he intends his
theory of disobedience to apply only to those that do. (As an
aside, he suggests that the wisdom of civil disobedience will be
problematic when there is no common conception of justice,
since disobedience may serve only to rouse the majority to
more repressive measures.)[1]

This is not the place to discuss Rawls's theory of justice as a
whole. I want to discuss only its application to our topic. From
his view that civil disobedience is justified by 'the principles of
justice which regulate the constitution and social institutions
generally', Rawls draws the consequence that 'in justifying
civil disobedience one does not appeal to principles of personal

[1] Ibid., pp. 386–7.

morality or to religious doctrines . . . Instead one invokes the commonly shared conception of justice which underlies the political order.'[1]

Even bearing in mind that this is intended to apply only to societies in which there is a common conception of justice, one can see that this is a serious limitation on the grounds on which disobedience can be justified. I shall suggest two ways in which this limitation could be unreasonable.

Firstly, if disobedience is an appeal to the community, why can it only be an appeal which invokes principles which the community already accepts? Why could one not be justified in disobeying in order to ask the majority to alter or extend the shared conception of justice? Rawls might think that it could never be necessary to go beyond this shared conception, for the shared conception is broad enough to contain all the principles necessary for a just society. Disobedience, he would say, can be useful to ensure that society does not depart too seriously from this shared conception, but the conception itself is unimpeachable. The just society, on this view, may be likened to a good piece of machinery: there may occasionally be a little friction, and some lubrication will then be necessary but the basic design needs no alteration.

Now Rawls can, of course, make this true by definition. We have already seen that he intends his theory of disobedience to apply only to societies which have a common conception of justice. If Rawls means by this that his theory applies only when the shared conception of justice encompasses all the legitimate claims that anyone in the society can possibly make, then it follows that no disobedience which seeks to extend or go beyond the shared conception of justice can be legitimate. Since this would follow simply in virtue of how Rawls had chosen to use the notion of a shared conception of justice, however, it would be true in a trivial way, and would be

[1] Ibid., p. 365.

utterly unhelpful for anyone wondering whether he would be justified in disobeying in an actual society.

If Rawls is to avoid this trivializing of his position it would seem that he must be able to point to at least some societies which he thinks have an adequate sense of justice. This course would invite our original question: why will disobedience be justified only if it invokes this particular conception of justice? This version of the theory elevates the conception of justice at present held by some society or societies into a standard valid for all time. Does any existing society have a shared conception of justice which cannot conceivably be improved? Maybe we cannot ourselves see improvements in a particular society's conception of justice, but we surely cannot rule out the possibility that in time it may appear defective, not only in its application, but in the fundamentals of the conception itself. In this case, disobedience designed to induce the majority to rethink its conception of justice might be justified.

I cannot see any way in which Rawls can avoid one or other of these difficulties. Either his conception of justice is a pure ideal, in which case it does not assist our real problems, or it unjustifiably excludes the use of disobedience as a way of making a radical objection to the conception of justice shared by some actual society.

Rawls's theory of civil disobedience contains a second and distinct restriction on the grounds of legitimate disobedience. As we have seen, he says that the justification of disobedience must be in terms of justice, and not in terms of 'principles of personal morality or religious doctrine'. It is not clear exactly what this phrase means, but since Rawls opposes it to 'the commonly shared conception of justice which underlies the political order' we may take it to include all views that are not part of this shared conception. This makes it a substantial restriction, since according to Rawls there are important areas of morality which are outside the scope of justice. The theory of justice is, he says, 'but one part of a moral view'.[1] As an example of an area of morality to which justice is inapplicable, Rawls instances our relations with animals. It is, he says, wrong to be cruel to animals, although we do not owe them justice. If we combine this view with the idea that the justification of civil disobedience must be in terms of justice, we can see that Rawls is committed to holding that no amount of cruelty to animals can justify disobedience. Rawls would no doubt admit that severe and widespread cruelty to animals would be a great moral evil, but his position requires him to say that the licensing, or even the promotion of such cruelty by a government (perhaps to amuse the public, or as is more likely nowadays, for experimental purposes) could not possibly justify civil disobedience, whereas something less serious would justify disobedience if it were contrary to the shared conception of justice. This is a surprising and I think implausible conclusion. A similar objection could be made in respect of any other area of morality which is not included under the conception of justice. Rawls does not give any other examples, although he suggests (and it is implied by his theory of justice) that our dealings with permanent mental defectives do not come under the ambit of justice.[2]

So far I have criticized Rawls's theory of disobedience because of certain restrictions it places on the kind of reason which can justify disobedience. My final comment is different. Rawls frequently writes as if it were a relatively simple matter to determine whether a majority decision is just or unjust. This, coupled with his view that the community has a common conception of justice, leads him to underestimate the importance of a settled, peaceful method of resolving disputes. It could also lead one to the view that there are cases in which the majority is clearly acting beyond its powers, that is, that there are areas of life in which the decision-procedure is entirely

[1] Ibid., p. 512.   [2] Ibid., p. 510.

without weight, for instance, if it tries to restrict certain freedoms. (This view is similar to that discussed earlier in connection with rights.) Consider the following passage:

It is assumed that in a reasonably just democratic regime there is a public conception of justice by reference to which citizens regulate their political affairs and interpret the constitution. The persistent and deliberate violation of the basic principles of this conception over any extended period of time, especially the infringement of the fundamental equal liberties, invites either submission or resistance. By engaging in civil disobedience a minority forces the majority to consider whether it wishes to have its actions construed in this way, or whether, in view of the common sense of justice, it wishes to acknowledge the legitimate claims of the minority.[1]

There will, of course, be some instances in a society when the actions of the majority can only be seen as a deliberate violation for selfish ends of basic principles of justice. Such actions do 'invite submission or resistance'. It is a mistake, though, to see these cases as in any way typical of those disputes which lead people to ask whether disobedience would be justified. Even when a society shares a common conception of justice, it is not likely to agree on the application of this conception to particular cases. Rawls admits that it is not always clear when the principles of justice have been violated, but he thinks it is often clear, especially when the principle of equal liberty (for Rawls the first principle of justice) is involved. As examples, he suggests that a violation of this principle can clearly be seen when 'certain religious groups are repressed' and when 'certain minorities are denied the right to vote or to hold office . . .'[2] These cases appear straightforward, but are they? Timothy Leary's League for Spiritual Discovery claimed to be a religious group using the drug LSD as a means of exploring ultimate spiritual reality. At least three other groups —the Neo-American Church, the Church of the Awakening,

[1] Ibid., pp. 365–6.   [2] Ibid., p. 372.

and the Native American Church—have used hallucinogenic drugs as part of religious ceremonies. Of these groups, only the last has legal permission to do so. Is freedom of worship being denied to the others? When is a group a religious group? There are similar problems about denying minorities the vote. Is the denial of the vote to children a violation of equal liberty? Or to convicted prisoners? It may seem obvious to us that these are legitimate exceptions, but then it seemed obvious to many respectable citizens a hundred years ago that blacks and women should not have the vote, and it seemed obvious to Locke that the suppression of atheism and Roman Catholicism were quite compatible with the principle of religious toleration.

When we go beyond religious persecution and the denial of voting rights, it is even easier to find complex disputes on which sincere disagreement over the justice of an action is likely to occur. Many of the issues which have led to civil disobedience in recent years have been of this more complex kind. This is why I do not think it helpful to assume that most issues arise from deliberate disregard of some common principles, or to try to specify limits, whether in the form of rights or of principles of justice, on what the majority can legitimately do.

CONSCIENTIOUS OBJECTION

I now want to discuss a commonly invoked justification of civil disobedience which is quite different from those so far considered, but which, because it also does not involve an attempt to coerce the majority into changing its decision, has been said to be consistent with democratic principles. I am referring to what is usually called 'conscientious objection', though as I hope to show, this is an unsuitable term. The conscientious objector seeks to ensure that, in the words of

Henry Thoreau: 'I do not lend myself to the wrong which I condemn.'[1] This form of disobedience, in so far as it is distinct from the forms already discussed, is undertaken in order to avoid taking part in the policies to which one objects, rather than in order to change those policies—though one may, and normally does, try to change the policies by legal means. This position is, of course, most commonly taken by those who refuse to serve in the armed forces. There is probably more general sympathy for this kind of disobedience than for any other. Yet discussion of it tends to be badly confused. In order to avoid possible confusions, I must begin by saying something about 'conscience' and what it is to have a conscientious objection to something.

People talk of 'conscience' in two main senses. Some mean by it something rather like a voice inside them which tells them what they ought to do and what they ought not to do, or if not a voice, then a feeling, often located (metaphorically?) in one's heart or the pit of the stomach. On this view, the dictates of conscience are given. They are data, and not the end-product of any process of rational consideration of the morally relevant features of the situation. It is even possible to say, using this sense of conscience: 'There are strong moral reasons in favour of breaking this promise, and the moral reasons against doing so seem to me to be much weaker, but my conscience still tells me that it would be wrong to break it.' If someone does say something like this, we may suspect that there is a psychological explanation for the judgements of his conscience—perhaps when he was young his mother drummed into him an abhorrence of promise-breaking under any circumstances—but even knowledge of such an explanation will not necessarily affect the content or strength of the inner voice or feeling. Conscience in this sense I will call 'traditional conscience'.[2]

[1] Bedau, *Civil Disobedience*, p. 35.
[2] The terminology I use in this section is that of A. Campbell Garnett,

According to the other important sense of conscience, a person acts according to his conscience, or conscientiously, when he acts on the basis of his own seriously thought out moral convictions. This has been called 'critical conscience' because it is the result of critical consideration of all the relevant moral factors. In particular, critical conscience subjects both conventional moral standards and the dictates of traditional conscience to criticism which, as far as possible, should be rational criticism. Usually when we describe an action as conscientious in the critical sense we do so in order to deny either that the agent was motivated by selfish desires, like greed or ambition, or that he acted on whim or impulse.

Bearing these two senses in mind, let us consider an oft-quoted passage from the essay by Thoreau, to which I have already referred:

Must the citizen ever for a moment, or in the least degree, resign his conscience to the legislator? Why has every man a conscience, then? I think we should be men first and subjects afterwards. It is not desirable to cultivate a respect for the law, so much as for the right. The only obligation which I have a right to assume, is to do at any time what I think right.[1]

If we take this passage to be referring to conscience in the traditional sense, the views expressed must be rejected. If we find that a law clashes with instinctive promptings, or feelings that, for all we know, are vestiges of our infantile dread of parental scoldings, we ought to give the considered judgement of the legislature some weight. This is especially true in a democratic society, for the reasons for which I have argued. To follow traditional conscience is to exclude the possibility that

---

'Conscience and Conscientiousness', in J. Feinberg (ed.), *Moral Concepts* (O.U.P., Oxford, 1969), pp. 80–92.

[1] Bedau, *Civil Disobedience*, p. 28. For a contemporary statement of a somewhat similar position, see R. P. Wolff, *In Defense of Anarchism* (Harper and Row, New York, 1970).

there may be moral reasons in favour of accepting the verdict of some form of decision-procedure, or at least, to refuse to give reasons of this sort any weight. A person who relied on traditional conscience in this way might even say: 'I can see that there are strong moral reasons in favour of obeying this decision, and the moral reasons against doing so seem to me to be much weaker, but my conscience still tells me that it would be wrong to obey.' To accept the dictates of traditional conscience in this way, without taking into consideration all relevant moral reasons, is to abdicate responsibility as a rational moral agent. Once we do take into consideration the fact that our action is contrary to law, however, we have passed from traditional conscience to critical conscience.

If we take Thoreau to be referring to critical conscience—an interpretation supported by the final sentence of the passage quoted—it is easy to accept his view, but it cannot possibly give us any guidance when we have to decide whether to obey a law. On this interpretation, the passage amounts only to the assertion that we should assess the rights and wrongs of obeying a law, and not obey laws without considering whether it is morally right to do so. It is compatible with this interpretation that in considering whether to obey or disobey a law we should always give very great weight to the fact that in disobeying we would be breaking a valid law, or rejecting a fair compromise, or refusing to accept the verdict of a decision-procedure in which we have participated. This is not really Thoreau's view, as other parts of the essay indicate, but nothing in the passage quoted counts against it, if the passage is about critical conscience. On this interpretation, the passage merely states the truism that the final decision on what to do must be up to the individual, and that this decision ought to be based on moral considerations. This is something which any authoritarian can admit, adding only that the individual ought morally, to regard the fact that an act would be illegal as an overriding moral reason against doing it. Someone else might say that the individual ought, morally, to give no weight to the fact that his act would be illegal. We can all agree that a man ought always to do what he thinks right—the real issue is when he should think it right to break the law.

The points that have emerged from this discussion of Thoreau are quite general in application. A responsible moral agent will not follow his traditional conscience automatically; and the fact that it would be against one's traditional conscience to do an act, were one *not* legally obliged to do it, does not mean that it must be against one's (critical) conscience to do it if one *is* legally obliged to do it. For legal obligation can be a relevant moral consideration, particularly, as I have argued, when it has arisen through the sort of democratic processes I described in the first part of this book. In some, though not all cases, this factor will 'tip the scales', altering a man's view of what, in conscience, he ought to do. In any case, the crucial point is that the advice 'follow your conscience' cannot provide any answers to the problem of what we ought to do, for our problem is, precisely, what action our (critical) conscience directs us to do. The verdict of critical conscience is our answer to the problem of what we ought to do, and our answer to this problem is the verdict of our (critical) conscience. A failure to understand this has marred much of what has been written about conscience and disobedience.[1]

Our discussion of conscience, then, has led to the conclusion that conscientious objection is either an unreflective act, not

[1] See, for example, D. Spitz, 'Democracy and the Problem of "Civil Disobedience"', *American Political Science Review*, vol. 48 (1954), pp. 386–403. Spitz thinks the dissenter's problem is whether to obey his conscience and break the law, or obey the law and violate his conscience, but in so far as the dissenter's problem is a moral problem, it is surely whether on reflection, his (critical) conscience is for or against obedience. If, after taking all the morally relevant factors into consideration, his conscience tells him to disobey there is no further moral question to ask.

the act of a responsible moral agent, or else no different, in so far as it is conscientious, from all the acts of disobedience discussed in this book, for they have all been motivated by moral considerations. (This is why, as I said earlier, I think the term 'conscientious objection' a poor way of distinguishing the particular kinds of disobedience with which we are here concerned.) The distinctive feature of the disobedience of the person usually called a 'conscientious objector' is conscientiousness only when he is contrasted with those who refuse for selfish or other less worthy motives to do what they are legally obliged to do. When the disobedience of the conscientious objector is contrasted with the other forms of disobedience we have been discussing, its distinctive feature is that it is neither an attempt to force the majority to alter its decision, nor an attempt to gain publicity, or to ask the majority to reconsider its decision. This means that although the action of the conscientious objector does not represent the kind of resort to force which is the antithesis of a democratic decision-procedure, it is also not the sort of act that can be justified on the grounds that it is designed to give effect to democratic ideals, such as fair compromise and equal concern for all, which have been neglected or distorted. The conscientious objector cannot plead that his disobedience is provisional, that he disobeys only to gain a fair hearing, or to prod the majority into reconsidering its decision, and that he will obey the decision of the majority once he has put his case, or the majority have considered their decision afresh. What then is his position with regard to the democratic reasons for obedience?

The position of the conscientious objector is, I think, that the reasons for obedience deriving from law and democracy constrain him against the use of illegal means to thwart the majority in carrying out the decision to which he objects, but are of insufficient weight to overcome the moral objections he has to 'lending himself to the injustice he condemns'. The conscientious objector endeavours to achieve some sort of balance between reasons for obeying the law and accepting democratic procedures, on the one hand, and other deeply held moral principles on the other. It is a position well suited to those who believe that it is worse to commit a wrong oneself than to fail to do one's utmost to prevent a wrong being done by another. This idea—that there is a significant moral distinction between overt acts and mere omissions—is widely held. It is enshrined in the aphorism: 'Thou shalt not kill, but needst not strive officiously to keep alive.' It lies behind the practice of doctors who allow a seriously deformed infant to die from an easily curable infection, but will not take any positive step aimed at terminating the life of the infant. It is hard to see any other justification, except a distinction between acts and omissions, for the fact that we do not see anything wrong in a wealthy man spending his money on luxuries instead of using it to save people from starvation in famine-prone areas. Nevertheless, it is difficult to see any rational justification for attributing much importance to the distinction. On utilitarian grounds it should be just as important to prevent something evil occurring as it is to refrain from doing evil myself. So the utilitarian who objects to, say, conscription for an unjustifiable war, will not be content with conscientious objection. He may refuse to fight himself, but he will think it equally important to stop others fighting. If he thinks he is justified in disobeying the law by refusing to fight he will also, other things being equal, think he is justified in disobeying the law in other ways that are likely to be equally effective in ending or reducing the fighting. For someone who does attribute great moral importance to the acts/omissions distinction, however, the position of a conscientious objector may be the best possible means of balancing the conflicting moral considerations with which one is faced when commanded by a democratic law to do what one believes to be very wrong.

The conscientious objector in a democratic society is in an awkward position. From the point of view of other members of a democratic society, the conscientious objector does not do what is required of him. From the point of view which leads him to disobey, he does not do everything possible to get a decision which he believes to be wrong rescinded or made inoperative. He may be accused of putting the purity of his own soul above the good of others. What is the good of refusing to, say, fight in an unjust war, if one knows that others are going to do so instead?

Despite these weaknesses, no form of disobedience is as widely respected as conscientious objection—although to say this is not to say much. The fact that many countries have made allowance for conscientious objectors in their conscription laws is evidence of this respect. The fact that scarcely any country considers conscientious objection to a particular war to be a ground for exemption from service in that war is evidence of the limits of this respect. There is no reason to think that the more specific objection is any less conscientious, and it seems to me to be the more rational position. To claim to know that there could never be any circumstances in which it is right to go to war seems to me unreasonable; on the other hand, to say of a particular war that it is unjustifiable will very often be both reasonable and correct. Why then should governments respect the conscientious views of the complete pacifist, but not those of the objector to a particular war? As should be obvious from our analysis of conscience, both views can be conscientious, in some sense. It is, if anything, more likely that the complete pacifist will base his position on traditional conscience—on, say, the feeling that it must always be wrong to kill—while the objector to a particular war, who must have assessed the relevant facts, is more likely to be acting according to critical conscience. Do the exemption provisions reveal a preference for traditional conscience over critical conscience? Could it be that governments are so badly confused about the nature of conscience that they simply equate it with traditional conscience? This possibility cannot be entirely discounted, but there are alternative explanations.

It is sometimes said that if governments allowed exemption to those who based their judgement on the particular facts of a war, this would in some way be allowing the objectors' assessments of the facts to prevail over the assessment of the government itself, thus giving legal recognition to the superiority of the dissentient views.[1] This is a dubious argument, for if allowing an objector's judgement of fact to excuse him from military service accorded legal recognition of the superiority of his views, allowing a pacifist's moral judgement to excuse him should have the same effect. It is in any case not true that to accept a judgement, whether of fact or morality, as a ground for exemption is to accord legal recognition to the soundness of that judgement. In fact, under the laws of most countries, the officials or judges responsible for exemptions are required to test sincerity of conviction, but not soundness of belief.

Perhaps the best argument that a government could put in defence of its refusal to grant exemption to those who object to a particular war is that so many people would fall into the category of those exempted that the armed forces would be significantly weakened. This sounds cynical, yet there is something to be said for it. Coercion is always in need of justification, and coercing a man to do something contrary to his most deeply held moral beliefs (which we normally encourage him to follow) requires special justification. Whenever possible, exemptions should be provided for those who refuse, on moral grounds, to comply with a law. In cases like the United Kingdom Abortion Act, such exemption (for doctors who object to performing abortions) is relatively easy to provide.

[1] See E. van den Haag, 'Civil Disobedience', *Quadrant* (Australia), April 1972, p. 50.

There are enough doctors without conscientious objections to do the requisite number of abortions. In other cases, no exemption at all may be possible. If simple hygiene laws controlling the disposal of rubbish and sewage waters are necessary to prevent the spread of disease, there cannot be exemptions for any who might have moral objections to observing hygienic precautions. This is an area in which non-observance by a very few can render useless the precautions taken by everyone else. Conscription in time of war probably falls in between these cases. It may be that if governments exempted all those who objected, there would not be enough men left to fight the war. From the point of view of the objectors, of course, this would be a good thing, but if the government is convinced that the war is necessary or just, it will give overriding priority to securing enough men to win the war. It is conceivable that the government will be right to do this, although the fact that so many have conscientious objections to the war should make the government very doubtful about whether the war is justified.

The arguments in favour of exempting non-pacifist conscientious objectors gain strong support from the experience of Great Britain in the Second World War—the only time, so far as I know, a nation at war has exempted people with political objections to the particular war being fought. Although there was some confusion at the beginning, because the statute exempting conscientious objectors from national service did not expressly refer to the grounds of objection, the Appellate Tribunals eventually granted exemption to, for instance, Indian nationalists who said they would fight to defend a free India, and to socialists who were ready to fight in a class war against capitalism, but not on behalf of 'imperialist powers'. Later, the Minister of Labour officially stated that the exemption of non-pacifists was in accordance with the intention of parliament. This policy was maintained throughout the desperate days after Dunkirk, when every available man was wanted. This tolerant attitude was apparently due partly to genuine respect for conscientious beliefs, partly to a desire to avoid a repetition of the disgraceful and ultimately futile persecution of conscientious objectors that occurred during the First World War, and partly to a judicious assessment of the value to the army of men bitterly opposed to the war they were supposed to be fighting. In any case, the policy never caused difficulties. The overwhelming majority of the population believed Britain was fighting a just war, and the number of men applying for exemption as conscientious objectors was never more than 2·2 per cent of the total number conscripted. After May 1940, the figure was never above 0·8 per cent. These figures include pacifists and non-pacifists. No separate records were kept, but non-pacifists appear to have been a tiny fraction of those applying.[1]

In recent years, the war in Vietnam has led some pacifists away from what is normally thought of as conscientious objection to such an extent that provisions in the law offering exemption from military service are spurned as 'a convenient way by which . . . resistance to conscription and the military . . . is effectively silenced'. People who would be eligible for exemption refuse to accept it on the grounds that to do so 'is to tacitly accept the legitimacy of the system of conscription and the military for which conscription exists'.[2] Those who

[1] See D. Hayes, *Challenge of Conscience: The Story of the Conscientious Objectors* (Allen & Unwin, London, 1949). I owe this reference to David Malament, 'Selective Conscientious Objection and the *Gillette* Decision', *Philosophy and Public Affairs*, vol. I, no. 4 (Summer 1972). This is the best discussion of the issue I have seen.

[2] R. M. Boardman, 'Letter to Local Board No. 114', reprinted in Bedau, *Civil Disobedience*, pp. 178–86. In the letter Boardman, a pacifist, tells his draft board why he cannot accept exemption as a conscientious objector. For another argument for non-compliance with exemption procedures, see A. J. Muste, *Of Holy Disobedience*, reprinted in part in Bedau, *Civil Disobedience*, pp. 135–45.

argue in this way are not, I think, merely expressing the point I made earlier, that from a utilitarian point of view it is just as important to prevent fighting as to refuse to fight oneself. They are arguing, rather, that to apply for, and be granted, exemption under the statutory procedures is too easy a way out. Instead, a pacifist should refuse to have anything to do with the law relating to conscription; and if necessary, he should go to gaol for his beliefs. Bertrand Russell expressed a similar feeling when, in the article from which I have already quoted, he went on to say:

Those of us who protest against nuclear weapons and nuclear war cannot acquiesce in a world in which each man owes such freedom as remains to him to the capacity of his government to cause many hundreds of millions of deaths by pressing a button. This is to us an abomination, and rather than seem to acquiesce in it we are willing, if necessary, to become outcasts and to suffer whatever obloquy and whatever hardship may be involved in standing aloof from the governmental framework.[1]

The idea behind what Russell is saying here, as well as behind the refusal of pacifists to accept exemption, is that it is the illegality of the act, the fact that it is an act of disobedience, which is essential, because to obey the law is to accept or acquiesce in conscription, or nuclear armaments, or whatever. This idea rests on a fundamental misunderstanding of the nature of democracy, a misunderstanding which illustrates once more the importance of a proper understanding of the basis of a democratic decision-procedure.[2] I do not think I need to repeat here what I have said before about democracy being a procedure for resolving disputes which depends for its

[1] Bedau, *Civial Disobedience*, pp. 158-9.
[2] A similar misunderstanding gives rise to the alleged paradox discussed by R. Wollheim in 'A Paradox in the Theory of Democracy' in P. Laslett and W. G. Runciman (eds.), *Philosophy, Politics and Society* second series, (Blackwell, Oxford, 1962).

existence on the disputants regarding the verdict of the decision-procedure as having substantial, though not overriding, moral weight because it is the result of the decision-procedure. If this is understood, it follows that obedience to a democratic decision is, at most, indicative of acceptance of the democratic system, and not of any military or nuclear 'system' set up by democratic procedures. If one uses all the means available under a democratic system to attempt to alter or abolish the military system, making one's opposition to the military as widely known as possible, then I do not think it can be said that one acquiesces or even seems to acquiesce in it. Those who think they must disobey democratic laws in order to avoid acquiescing, or seeming to acquiesce, in particular results of the democratic system are mistaken: their actions are really indicative of a refusal to acquiesce in the democratic system itself.

PART III

FROM MODEL TO REALITY

IN the previous sections, in arguing that there are special reasons for obeying the law in a democratic society, I deliberately avoided spelling out what I meant by 'democratic'. I was able to do this because I was arguing from simplified models. Whatever controversies there may be about the nature of democracy, I think no one will deny that my third model can properly be described as democratic. If the conclusions we have reached by discussing these models are to have any application to the real world, however, we must ask to what extent they apply to existing full-size political communities.

DEMOCRACY, DIRECT AND REPRESENTATIVE

First, to recapitulate those features of the third model association that gave rise to the reasons for obedience applicable to the third model only: the association decided issues by a vote of the assembled members, the majority view prevailing; every member's vote counted equally; the meetings were conducted according to impartial procedural rules, and the votes tallied accurately; any member could propose a motion and there was, within the procedural rules, complete freedom to speak for or against any proposal; the majority did not use its numerical superiority to exploit any minority.

Democracy, as the *Concise Oxford Dictionary* defines it, means '(State practising) government by the people, direct or representative.' My third model is a form of direct democracy. The members themselves take the decisions about how their community is to be organized. Direct democracy can claim to be the basic form of democracy, both historically and conceptually. Historically, Western democratic thought goes back to Athens in the fifth century B.C. In the Athenian city-state at that time, the citizens met in a General Assembly and there, under conditions of political equality and free debate, discussed and voted on the major issues that faced the community. Admittedly, not all those who lived in Athens were citizens in the legal sense, and it is sometimes said (though just as often denied) that Athenian citizens would not have had the leisure demanded by their political system, were it not for the existence of slavery. I do not know whether there is any truth in this claim. In any case, within the limits of its qualifications for citizenship, the Athenian system was an example of direct democracy like our third model association. Whatever obligations exist in this third model would also exist in a direct democracy.

Conceptually, too, direct democracy is the basic form of democracy. The idea of representative democracy implies representatives who 'take the place of' or 'are present instead of' others. Representative democracy is therefore in virtue of the meaning of the term a substitute for something else, and this something else can only be direct democracy. The question we are going to have to ask about this substitute is whether the reasons for obedience that hold in a direct democracy also hold in a representative democracy. Before we consider this question directly, however, let us ask a more general question: why accept a substitute at all?

One of the most common platitudes in political theory, repeated in all the elementary textbooks, is that while direct democracy might be all very well in a small city-state, it is obviously quite unrealistic in a nation-state of several million people. In fact, this platitude is certainly false. With the communications technology available to us today, an extension of

Athenian-style democracy to a modern state would be perfectly feasible. Without going into details, it is easy to envisage vote-recording devices installed in private homes and public places, linked to a central computer and operated by means of some personalized device, like those already in use for obtaining cash from the automatic machines outside banks. Proposals could be debated on radio and television, and the public could contribute by telephone—not everyone, of course, but then not everyone could contribute in Athens. If, then, we have not seized the opportunity provided by technological advances to restore democracy to its purest form, it must be because for one reason or another we are unenthusiastic about such a restoration. Maybe people would find it inconvenient to vote frequently, or consider themselves incompetent to express an opinion on major issues, or perhaps those who are influential in forming opinion on these matters are apprehensive about the decisions that might emerge from direct popular votes on issues relating to racial equality, capital punishment, or foreign policy.

Looking at the matter historically, however, we must concede this much truth to the common platitude: representative systems came into existence at a time when it was impossible for all the citizens of the state to take collective decisions directly. Nation-states cover many more people, and much greater territory, than the Greek city-states. So those who could not go to a central meeting sent others to go in their place. This leads us to the most straightforward of the various theories of representation. It is the theory suggested by taking the term literally. The representative is to speak and vote as those he is representing would have spoken and voted, had they been able to be present.[1] Representation, on this view, is a

[1] For examples of this view, see H. Pitkin, *The Concept of Representation* (University of California Press, Los Angeles and Berkeley, 1967), p. 276.

device for producing a system of government differing from direct democracy only in so far as is inevitable if it is to operate effectively in a large society without a sophisticated communications network.

There are, however, difficulties in this notion of a representative doing as those he represents would have done. If the citizen wants something (say, lower taxes) which the representative knows to be incompatible with other things the citizen wants (more schools) but the citizen does not appreciate this incompatibility, what is the representative to do? The citizen, if he were present, would vote for both lower taxes and more schools, but the representative can hardly do this. Even greater difficulties arise when we consider that the representative is taking the place not of one citizen, but of a considerable number, with a variety of opinions. Quite apart from the minority who did not vote for the candidate who obtained the most votes, there will be differences of opinion among those who did vote for him.

These and related difficulties have led some thinkers, most notably Rousseau, to deny that the people can be represented. Others have insisted that the difficulties arise only on a mistaken view of what a representative should be, and have therefore offered alternative accounts of what a representative should be. While Rousseau rejected representation because he believed 'will cannot be represented'[1] Edmund Burke told his electors: 'If government were a matter of will upon any side, yours without question ought to be superior. But government and legislation are matters of reason and judgement.'[2] Burke's view that the member of parliament, once elected, is free to

[1] J.-J. Rousseau, *The Social Contract*, trans. G. Hopkins, in *Social Contract*, ed. E. Barker (O.U.P., London, 1947), Bk. III, ch. 15.
[2] E. Burke, 'Speech to the Electors of Bristol' (1774) in *The Works of Edmund Burke* (Bohn's standard Library, George Bell and Sons, London, 1886), vol. I, p. 447.

exercise his own judgement, independently of the desires of his electors, is often cited in defence of parliamentary decisions which are contrary to public opinion. The electors, on this view, are voting for the man they think will make the best decisions, rather than for a man who will express their own opinions or promote their own interests.

Another means of overcoming difficulties in the idea of the representative doing as his constituents would have done is the suggestion that the representative body 'should be an exact portrait, in miniature, of the people at large, as it should think, feel, reason, and act like them'.[1]

Fortunately, we do not have to decide which of these and other possible theories of representation we prefer. We are interested in whether the obligations of a direct democracy continue to hold under these systems of representation. The central questions, here, are firstly whether these systems are fair compromises between competing claims to power, and secondly whether there is the opportunity for voluntary participation in the decision-procedure which would give rise to a quasi-consensual obligation.

On the first question, none of the theories of representation mentioned above necessarily involves a departure from fair compromise. If the general meeting is a fair compromise between competing claims to power in a small society, giving no advantage to any individual or faction, these representative systems could all function so as to give no advantages to individuals or factions in a larger society.[2] This would clearly

[1] John Adams, quoted in H. Pitkin, *The Concept of Representation*, p. 60.

[2] As in the model, 'no advantages' can only mean 'no inbuilt advantages'. Just as, in the model, taking decisions at meetings gave an advantage to the most persuasive speakers, so in a larger society there could be incidental advantages for some, for instance, for those who control the major newspapers and television stations. The extent to which this destroys the democratic reasons for obedience has already been discussed on pp. 74-80 above.

be the case if representatives really could vote as those who elected them would have voted, had they been present and properly informed; it would also apply if the assembly of representatives was a genuine microcosm of society as a whole (a result more likely to be produced by proportional representation than by the simple majority systems of voting used in Great Britain and the United States). It is perhaps more doubtful if Burke's view satisfies the fair compromise requirement. It would satisfy it if everyone had the opportunity to vote for a representative in whose judgement he had confidence; if, however, there were some who could find no candidate they trusted, they would be at a disadvantage, and might see no point in voting at all. Burke could reply that one is always free to stand oneself, but practical considerations may make this a purely theoretical freedom.

As for the second question, does voting count as voluntary participation in the decision, giving rise to a quasi-consensual obligation to accept the verdict? Once again the answer, in theoretical terms, is affirmative. The election of representation plays an important part in the decision-making procedure. People who take part in the electoral process are in general prepared to accept the decisions indirectly reached through that process. As in direct democracy, that there should be acceptance in normal cases follows from the meaning or point of voting. Therefore people voting have a reasonable expectation that others will accept the result as they themselves intend to do. There is, however, one way in which a representative democracy may destroy this obligation which could not occur in a direct democracy. If the representative, after election, were to act in a manner contrary to the way he had lead those who elected him to believe he would act, the obligation created by participation would no longer hold. Thus, assuming we are operating under the literal understanding of representation, if people voted for a man who said he would vote for proposals

X, Y, and Z because, had they been able to attend the assembly, they would have voted for these proposals; and the representative then votes against X, Y, and Z, the people may well maintain that their votes were obtained by a kind of fraud, and that they are therefore under no obligation to accept the outcome. The same point would apply to the microcosmic theory if, for instance, the elected representative of a group of factory workers were to throw off his overalls after the election and reveal himself as the son of the factory-owner. If representatives are to be independent of those who elected them, as Burke thought they should be, it seems less likely that conduct after an election could invalidate the election itself. One way in which it could still happen would be if, in order to show that he was the man that could best be trusted to make the right decisions, the candidate had indicated how he would vote on certain issues if elected, and then later voted differently without claiming that circumstances had altered.

All this is still abstract theory. I have suggested that there are forms of representative democracy in which the reasons for obedience that hold in a direct democracy would still have their full force. In theory, the transition to a larger society need not vitiate these reasons. But none of this has any immediate bearing on the societies in which we live. These societies (I am assuming that the reader lives in one of the countries governed by some form of parliamentary democracy) are not regulated by the prescriptions of any pure theory of representation. Their institutions have been shaped by a great many other factors. Yet it is in reference to these societies that so many people say: 'Disobedience in a democracy is (almost) never justified.' We have not completed our examination of this idea until we have considered the application of the democratic reasons for obedience to these 'Western democracies'.

CONTEMPORARY WESTERN DEMOCRACY

To what extent do the political systems of those states we in the West commonly think of as democracies—Britain, the United States, France, Australia, India, Japan, and so on—incorporate the prerequisites of the democratic reasons for obedience? To answer this question we must take note of the findings of contemporary political scientists. Naturally, these writers differ among themselves about how well modern democracies work. It would be easy, if we were to select our descriptions from those most hostile to the Western method of government, to come to the conclusion that these political systems, far from being fair compromises, are in reality the means by which one class disguises its oppression of the other. This approach, however, would convince only those already hostile to Western democracy. So I shall, instead, rely on descriptions of Western democracy given by those who count themselves among its supporters.

Although differing on many points, those who have written about modern democratic forms of government tend to agree that the traditional theories of representative democracy do not describe any existing national political system. Representatives do not vote as their constituents would have voted; nor do electors choose those whose wise judgement they feel they can trust; nor are representative bodies microcosms of the nation. All these theories, contemporary writers say, unrealistically attribute to ordinary people informed opinions on the major issues of the day, or on the personal characteristics of candidates for electoral office. In no large-scale society do the great mass of the people have such opinions. Some writers would add: it is a good thing that they do not. These writers, as I have said, are not enemies of democracy. They regard themselves as its supporters. The man who did more than anyone else to gain acceptance for this revised view of democracy was Joseph Schumpeter, who served as Minister of Finance in a Social-Democrat Government in Austria after the First World War. and quit a professorship in Berlin to go to America when Nazism was beginning to assert itself in Germany. Earlier writers, notably Mosca and Pareto, had criticized classical democratic theory along similar lines, but it was only with Schumpeter's *Capitalism, Socialism, and Democracy* (first published in 1942) that these ideas began to take hold among democrats. The book contains a forthright attack on the 'myths' of democracy, including the belief that '. . . "the people" hold a definite and rational opinion about every individual question and that they give effect to this opinion—in a democracy—by choosing "representatives" who will see to it that that opinion is carried out.'[1] In place of this myth of classical democratic theory, Schumpeter proposes a more realistic revision:

Voters do not decide issues. But neither do they pick their members of parliament from the eligible population with a perfectly open mind. In all normal cases the initiative lies with the candidate who makes a bid for the office of member of parliament and such local leadership as that may imply. Voters confine themselves to accepting this bid in preference to others or refusing to accept it.[2]

It should be noted that Schumpeter is going beyond what Burke said about the independence of the candidate, once elected. Burke did not deny that voters have a real and un-limited choice as to whom they shall elect; according to Schum-peter, however, the initiative lies with the candidate, not the voters, and the voter's choice is limited to accepting one of the small number of 'bids' made to him.

Strong support for the view that it is unrealistic to expect voters to do more than accept one of a very limited number of

[1] 3rd ed. (Allen and Unwin, London, 1961), p. 269.
[2] *Capitalism, Socialism, and Democracy*, p. 282.

options has come from studies of how people vote. Surveys of voting behaviour have found that very few voters are properly informed about the issues at stake in elections; in particular, the minority who change their vote between elections (and so effectively determine the outcome of elections) are generally less well informed than the average voter, and vote on the basis of factors normally considered trivial or irrelevant.[1] These results could, of course, have been taken as an indication that real democracy is yet to be achieved; instead, most post-war democratic theorists, clinging to the idea that if 'democracy' has any meaning at all, then the United States, Britain, and nations with similar political systems must be democracies, have argued that the voting studies make obsolete traditional ideas about the role of the people in a democracy. It would be tedious to illustrate this with quotations from even a sample of the writers who have taken this position.[2] Instead I shall, in the following discussion, rely mainly on the work of Robert Dahl, a well-known and generally middle-of-the-road representative of modern American writers on democracy. Dahl accepts Schumpeter's criticism of traditional ideas about democracy, in so far as he believes that:

A good deal of democratic theory leads us to expect more from national elections than they can possibly provide. We expect elections to reveal the 'will' or the preferences of a majority on a set of issues. This is one thing elections rarely do, except in an almost trivial fashion . . . Elections and political competition do not make for government by majorities in any very significant way, but they vastly increase the size, number, and variety of minorities whose

[1] Of these studies, perhaps the best known is that by B. Berelson, P. Lazarsfeld, and W. McPhee. *Voting* (University of Chicago Press, Chicago, 1954).

[2] For an excellent brief analysis of the most notable of these, see P. Bachrach *The Theory of Democratic Elitism* (Athlone Press, London, 1969) to which the present discussion is indebted.

preferences must be taken into account by leaders in making policy choices.[1]

I shall accept the consensus of political scientists that these views describe, far better than the traditional theory of democracy, what actually happens in a modern state of the type we know as Western democracy. I shall not discuss in detail the claims made that in important respects modern democracy is a better system than traditional-style democracy would be. Our concern is with reasons for obeying the law and not with the virtues of different political systems. Nevertheless, as I argued towards the end of Part I, one reason for obeying the laws of a political system is that one prefers that system to any other, and desires to support it. In this connection we can note that in giving up the notion of effective mass participation the new theories also give up an aim that J. S. Mill thought very important, the aim of self-development through participation in the government of one's community. Against this we must balance, if the revisionists are right, certain advantages: stability, élitist restraint of mass 'stampedes',[2] protection for some (though not all) minorities against majority tyranny,[3] and flexibility.[4] The political systems described by the revisionist writers also save us time and inconvenience, in that less of us have to concern ourselves with political issues. Despite these advantages, there is little doubt in my mind that these writers have made virtues out of necessity. The political system they describe may be better than any other existing political system. It may even be the best workable system a large nation-state could have. This, no doubt, is what the revisionists believe, and so they think it important that we should not be tempted to

[1] University of Chicago Press, Chicago, 1956, pp. 131–2.

[2] Schumpeter, *Capitalism, Socialism, and Democracy*, p. 283; G. Sartori, *Democratic Theory* (Praeger, New York, 1965), p. 119.

[3] Dahl, *A Preface to Democratic Theory*, pp. 132, 151.

[4] Berelson, Lazarsfeld, and McPhee, *Voting*, pp. 316–22.

abandon or alter the system we have for the sake of the ideals of traditional democratic theory. Whether a closer approximation to these ideals would be workable is something about which we cannot be certain. If we think that the system we have is as good a political system as human beings possibly can have, we will see this as a reason for supporting, and therefore obeying the verdict of, this system. If, on the other hand, we believe the ideals of democratic theory both workable and worth striving for, we may take the findings of the voting studies simply as an indication of the distance still to be covered in realizing these ideals.

Of more direct concern to us is the question whether democracies, on the revised view of them, give rise to the two major reasons for obedience to law which held for democracies like our model democratic association, and for representative forms of government as they have been conceived in theories of representation. Firstly, we must ask, is the new democracy a fair compromise between all individuals and groups, giving no particular advantage to any of them?

According to earlier ideas of democracy, fairness is achieved by the institution of elections, in which each member of the society has one vote, which he allots to the candidate who he believes will best represent his views, interests, or social group, or who will make the best decisions on the major issues of the day. We have already seen that Schumpeter and Dahl deny that elections function in any of these ways. It is clear that it does not follow from the fact that everyone has a vote in an election that the election is a fair indication of the preferences of the electorate. It may not be a fair indication if, as Schumpeter suggests, voters are confined to accepting one of a small number of bids. This is the case when voters are, for all practical purposes, limited to a choice between two major parties. The theory of representative democracy developed in a time when there were no political parties in the modern sense, and it has been found difficult to reconcile the existence of parties with democratic presuppositions. As one writer has observed: 'while British political practice is now dominated by the assumption that the Parliamentary parties will behave as disciplined blocks, British political thought still lacks any justification of party discipline that is generally accepted.'[1] One might well think that whenever voters are limited to a choice between two or three major parties, views not represented by these parties are unfairly excluded. Before reaching this conclusion, however, it is necessary to consider the nature of political parties and the role they play in the democratic process, for there have been attempts to show that this role is compatible with democratic principles of equality.

In this book *Pluralist Democracy in the United States: Conflict and Consent*,[2] Dahl has a chapter entitled 'Political Parties: Contributions to Democracy'. In the course of this discussion Dahl concedes that 'A voter presented with two rival candidates might prefer neither of them so much as a third possible candidate who failed to win a nomination by either party.'[3] Dahl defends the party system by the following argument:

The fact remains, then, that whenever a diversity of viewpoints and desired alternatives exists among the citizens of a democracy, the citizens must, sooner or later, by one process or another, reject all but one alternative (even if the final choice is, in effect, the null alternative of inaction). There is no escaping this process; it is the essence of 'rationality', the only question is where and how it takes place. Much of the process of winnowing out alternatives could take place *before* an election, or *in* the election itself, or in negotiations

[1] A. H. Birch, *Representative and Responsible Government* (Allen and Unwin, London, 1964), p. 121; quoted in A. H. Birch, *Representation*, (Pall Mall, London, 1971), p. 100.

[2] Rand McNally, Chicago, 1967.

[3] Ibid., p. 251.

after the election. All party systems do some winnowing *before* an
election, making the *election* itself more decisive by reducing the
alternatives, thus leaving less winnowing to be done after the
election by bargaining and negotiation among members of different
parties . . .

The notion, then, that parties increase irrationality in making
choices by reducing the alternatives is based upon too simple a
picture of the processes by which collective political decisions can
be made, for all such processes necessarily involve a drastic reduction
in the alternatives. Although the question is obviously exceedingly
complex, it seems much more reasonable to conclude (as most
students of party do) that on the whole the parties play a beneficial
role in this process.[1]

Obviously Dahl is right to say that the process of reducing
alternative policies to one policy must be done somewhere;
what is curious, especially in view of the title of the chapter in
which this passage appears, is his apparent indifference whether
this reduction takes place before, in, or after an election. Surely
if the political system is to operate democratically, it will be
best if the reduction of alternatives takes place in the election
itself, so that all citizens participate equally in it, instead of
being presented with a *fait accompli* that leaves them little
meaningful choice in the election. The next best would perhaps
be if the reduction of alternatives were done after the election,
so that it is done by the elected representatives of the voters.
If, however, it is thought that unless a great deal of reduction
is done before the election the voters will be faced with too
complex and confusing a series of choices, then it would at
least be essential that this prior reduction of alternatives is
done in a democratic manner. In a modern party system of
democracy, this could occur only if political parties were
democratically organized. Dahl's indifference to how the
reduction of alternatives takes place is made even more puzzling

[1] Ibid., p. 252. Emphasis in original.

by his views on this matter. Discussing the criticism that parties are 'internally undemocratic and are ruled by oligarchies', Dahl readily concedes:

The charge is in considerable measure true. That the nominations and policies of political parties tend to be controlled by leaders, rather than the rank and file of members or registered supporters, seems undeniable. There is . . . more decentralization and diffusion of control in the two American parties than in many European parties; even so, both the Democratic and Republican parties would be more accurately described as coalitions of oligarchies than as democratic organizations.[1]

The picture that emerges is one of elections which present the citizen with a choice of two, or perhaps three or four, alternative policies and candidates, the selection of alternatives to be presented to the citizens being made by oligarchical organizations. It is hard to see how this can satisfy the requirement of fair compromise. Those who have influence in the major political parties possess far more power than fair compromise would allow them.

A democratic process dominated by two or three major parties is unlikely to be fair even when the parties genuinely differ, for the combinations of policies that they present are still 'package deals', and may not be those which the voters would prefer, were they free to select some policies from one party and others from another. When the policies of the major parties do not differ at all, or differ only insignificantly, the unfairness created by the dominance of parties becomes greater

[1] p. 245. This verdict is echoed by many students of political parties in other modern democracies. S. H. Beer, for example, summarizes one of the findings of his *Modern British Politics: A Study of Parties and Pressure Groups* (2nd ed., Faber and Faber, London, 1969) as follows: 'As has often been observed, the mass party, even if its inspiration is highly democratic, tends to separate leadership from the rank and file and to accumulate influence in the hands of an elite.' (p. 405.)

still. I have already mentioned, in a different context, the 1968 election for the Presidency of the United States. Although a substantial proportion of the population was opposed to the continuation of the war in Vietnam, the election gave this opposition no real opportunity to express itself, or to campaign and attempt to win influence in decision-making. Under these conditions, an election cannot be regarded as a fair compromise, for those in favour of continuing the war had the enormous advantage of controlling both the major political parties. In a less dramatic way, the same sort of thing happens whenever, in a two-party system, both parties agree on an issue.

Schumpeter, with characteristic frankness, acknowledges the unfairness of the party system when he says that his definition of democracy allows ways of competing for the peoples' votes which are 'strikingly analogous to the economic phenomena we label "unfair" or "fraudulent" competition or restraint of trade'. Schumpeter defends this by saying:

we cannot exclude them because if we did we should be left with a completely unrealistic ideal. Between this ideal case which does not exist and the cases in which all competition with the established leader is prevented by force, there is a continuous range of variation within which the democratic method of government shades off into the autocratic one by imperceptible steps. But if we wish to understand and not to philosophize, this is as it should be.[1]

Schumpeter, of course, is entitled to prefer understanding to philosophizing, but once we ask whether we ought to obey a law, we cannot avoid philosophizing (in the sense in which this whole book is a piece of philosophizing). In answering this question the difference between a fair and an unfair system may be more significant than the difference between a dictatorship and what Schumpeter would call a democracy.

In view of these acknowledged shortcomings of elections in

[1] *Capitalism, Socialism, and Democracy*, p. 271.

many Western democracies, it is not surprising that political theorists have looked to other aspects of these societies in order to show that the system is not really as unfair as consideration of elections alone might lead us to believe. According to many recent writers, the preferences of ordinary members of the public become politically significant not by means of elections, but only when they are organized into pressure groups. These groups bring their influence to bear on the government, and the course the government takes is, within broad limits, an attempt to satisfy the pressure groups and thus, indirectly, to put into effect the preferences of the members of the groups. This system could be a fair compromise, but only if it worked so as to give any individual the same influence, or at least the same opportunity for having influence, as any other individual.

Dahl thinks the role of minority groups vitally important in the politics of a country such as the United States—so important, in fact, that he sometimes refers to the American system of government as a 'polyarchy'. It is, he thinks, mainly the distinction between rule by a minority and rule by minorities which constitutes the difference between a democracy and a dictatorship:

. . . if there is anything to be said for the processes that distinguish democracy (or polyarchy) from dictatorship, it is not discoverable in the clear-cut distinction between government by a majority and government by a minority. The distinction comes much closer to being one between government by a minority and government by *minorities*. As compared with the political processes of a dictatorship, the characteristics of polyarchy greatly extend the number, size and diversity of the minorities whose preferences will influence the outcome of governmental decisions.[1]

Later, Dahl defines the 'normal' American political process as one 'in which all the active and legitimate groups in the popula-

---

[1] *A Preface to Democratic Theory*, p. 133. Emphasis in original.

tion can make themselves heard at some crucial stage in the process of decisions'.[1]

Does this mean that the normal American political system, assuming Dahl's description to be accurate, is a fair compromise? Not quite. We must examine the significance of the qualifying phrase 'active and legitimate' in order to see what groups cannot make themselves heard effectively. To take first 'active'. One might think that if a group is inactive, this is an indication that it cannot care very much about having influence on the government. If this were so, the exclusion of inactive groups would not matter much. It might even be desirable, as a means of taking into account not only numbers, but also the intensity with which people want to see their preferences expressed in government decisions. So long as every group has the opportunity to be active, the requirements of fair compromise may well be satisfied. Unfortunately, this is not what Dahl means. An inactive group, for him, is not necessarily a group which cannot be bothered to be active. A group may be inactive, he acknowledges, 'by free choice, violence, intimidation, or law'.

The qualification 'legitimate' is just as serious a restriction: 'By "legitimate" I mean those whose activity is accepted as right and proper by a preponderant portion of the active. In the South, Negroes were not until recently an active group. Evidently, Communists are not now a legitimate group.'[2] Thus groups may be denied the opportunity of being heard effectively because violence, intimidation, or law prevent them from being active, or because their activity, for some reason or other, is not accepted as right and proper by the active majority. It is clear that no justification, in terms of fair compromise, can be given for such exclusions. The groups excluded in these ways, therefore, would not have the special reason for obeying

[1] Ibid., pp. 137–8.
[2] Ibid., p. 138.

the law which exists in a model democracy, based on fair compromise.

There are other ways in which a pressure group system is unlikely to be fair to all members of society. As Dahl readily admits: 'To be "heard" covers a wide range of activities . . . Clearly, it does not mean that every group has equal control over the outcome . . . neither individuals nor groups are political equals.'[1] It is indeed obvious to anyone who reflects on the way pressure groups operate that they are anything but equal in influence (I mean by this, as I presume Dahl does, in proportion to their numbers). Some quite small groups, for instance, those representing big business, are in a favourable position. They have the money to contribute significantly to party funds, and to establish full-time public relations bureaux to put their point of view. They are more likely than other groups to have personal contacts with leading politicians, since they will tend to come from the same social strata, to have attended the same schools and colleges, belong to the same golf or social club, have professional contacts, and so on. Much larger groups, such as the consumers, will find it harder to get organized, contribute to party funds, or contact politicians. They may succeed eventually, if they are large enough, by making the issue electorally important. For other groups, however, with neither the influence of the small, highly organized group, nor the size of a group like the consumers, there may be no way in which they can make themselves heard effectively. The poor, for example, cannot organize properly as a pressure group, and are not numerous enough to have national electoral significance. These defects mean that the political system is permanently, or for long periods, biased against certain sections of the community. If these sections should find themselves faced with a law which they opposed,

[1] Ibid., p. 145. See also Dahl, *Pluralist Democracy in the United States*, Pt. IV.

but was passed because of the disproportionate influence of other groups, they cannot be urged to obey on the grounds that the pressure group system is a fair compromise.

We may conclude that modern democracies, as described by those favourable to this system of government, are not fair compromises between all competing groups and individuals. To say this is not to say that from this point of view there is no difference between a modern democracy and a dictatorship. We must agree with Dahl when he says that the former is ruled by more, larger, and more diverse minority groups than the latter. This means that there will be more groups, and more members of groups, who have had at least the share of influence on decisions that they would receive under a fair compromise. These people will have the same reason for obedience that they would have in a model democracy, in which there was fair compromise, since they will have had at least as much influence as they would have had in a model democracy. But those people who are deprived of the share of influence on decisions they would have had under a fair compromise do not have this basic reason for obedience. In respect of this particular reason for obedience, these people are in the same position as they would be if they were living under a dictatorship.

We have found that the first of the reasons for obedience which differentiated our model democratic association from our model dictatorships is not wholly applicable in a modern 'Western democracy'. What of the second reason, arising from participation? Although, as we have seen, elections in a modern democracy are not a fair means of taking decisions, this does not mean that participation in them cannot give rise to a reason for accepting the result. The reason, or obligation, arising from participation in the decision-procedure does not depend on the procedure being fair in all respects. It depends only on the procedure being fair in those respects in which the participant takes it to be fair. There is an analogy here with an agreement to take a dispute to a referee. If Smith and Jones should agree to settle a dispute between them by taking it to Smith's brother for arbitration, the relationship between Smith and the proposed referee being known to Jones at the time, Jones cannot later be heard to say that he is under no obligation to accept the verdict because the referee, being Smith's brother, must have been biased. This may be a ground for refusing to accept the proposed referee in the first place, but it does not affect the significance of accepting the referee if one nevertheless chooses to do so. Similarly, a person who participated in the 1968 United States presidential election cannot afterwards escape his obligation to accept the result of the election on the grounds that the election was unfair to opponents of the war. This too is a reason for not participating in the election, but it cannot vitiate the *prima facie* obligation to which participation gives rise, since the participant must have known that there was no anti-war candidate supported by either of the major parties. Even if one participated because there was nothing better to do, because one thought one candidate a more moderate supporter of the war than the other, so that one might do some good by voting for him, while one could achieve nothing by abstaining, the obligation would arise because (as I argued in Part I) it does not depend on actual consent. Matters of which the participant could not reasonably have been expected to be aware are, of course, different. Just as the discovery that Smith had bribed his brother would negate Jones's obligation to accept the verdict of Smith's brother, so the discovery of false ballot papers, or substantial miscounting, would negate the obligation which would otherwise arise from participation in the election.

These points seem to be fairly clear. Others are less easy to deal with briefly. There is difficulty in deciding just what one consents to when one participates in an election. We can say, simply enough, that one consents to abide by the result of the election, but what is the 'result of the election'? The result of, say, the 1970 General Election in Great Britain was that the Conservative Party gained a majority in Parliament and formed a government. So a participant in the election has a *prima facie* obligation to accept that the Conservatives ought to govern. But does this mean that he is similarly obliged to accept every law passed by the Conservatives? Not necessarily. A person who participates in an election is obliged as if he had consented to the stated policies of whatever party gains a majority being put into practice, but if the victorious party were to act in a manner contrary to all it had said prior to the election, I think the obligation would not hold. For the victorious party would then be in a position of power by means of deceit. The extreme example of this kind of deceit would be a member of one party declaring, after he had been elected with the support of that party, that he really favoured the policies of the other party. To do this would be to win by deceit as surely as if one had forged ballot papers, since the victory would come about only because the electors had been deceived. Actual cases, however, are invariably less clear-cut, and it is much more difficult to establish if an apparent inconsistency between promise and performance vitiates the obligation to accept the results of the election. Allowance must be made for changed circumstances, in which a change of policies may be necessary. To take an actual example, Dr. Benjamin Spock has argued that the nature of the democratic process in America does not oblige him to obey the law; he argues this on the ground that in the 1964 presidential election he personally campaigned for, and voted for, Lyndon B. Johnson because Johnson had promised to de-escalate the war in Vietnam—yet Johnson, after his election victory, continued the escalation of the war.[1] Spock, it

[1] In a B.B.C. interview broadcast 8 July 1970. The fact that Spock

seems to me, has a serious case here, along the lines we have just been discussing. To settle the issue, we would need to check two things: how definite a commitment to de-escalation did Johnson give? and did circumstances alter, significantly and unexpectedly, after the election in such a way as to make it reasonable for a man, who in previous circumstances had planned to de-escalate, to feel that he should, in the new conditions, continue to escalate? Neither of these questions is easy to answer, but if we did have answers to them we could, I think, decide whether Johnson's pre-election statements about Vietnam misled some voters as to the kind of candidate they were voting for. If we decided that this was the case, it would vitiate any *prima facie* obligation to obey Johnson's policies which those who participated in the election would otherwise have.

The position is in some respects similar when a victorious party introduces new proposals of a far-reaching kind which have not been put to the electorate (excluding, of course, measures designed to deal with a situation unforeseen at the time of the election). The theory that an 'electoral mandate' is necessary for such change has become popular in Britain since the war. In the year following the General Election of 1970, leading members of the Conservative Government made use of this idea in an attempt to discourage opposition to their proposals on industrial relations. Whatever one's attitude to the Industrial Relations Act, the Conservatives were justified in pointing out that they had indicated in their election manifesto what they would do, and I would agree that this was a relevant consideration against illegal opposition to the Act. If Dahl and the other revisionists are right in their descriptions of our form of government, however, the significance of this

---

campaigned personally makes little difference to the substance of his claim—it only makes it more graphic.

consideration is not that the election result showed that a majority of the adults in Britain supported the new law—many may have voted for the government in ignorance of, or even in spite of, this particular proposal. Rather, I believe, the prior announcement of Conservative intentions made illegal resistance by those who participated in the election harder to justify because by their participation they were obliged as if they had consented to these intentions being put into effect, should the Conservatives gain a majority.

The conclusion to be drawn from this discussion, in which we have assumed that modern Western democracy functions more or less as Dahl and similar political theorists have said it does, is that the specifically democratic reasons for obeying the law which applied in our model democratic community apply only in part to the societies in which we live. The discrepancy is a serious one. Many groups and individuals, not having an equal share of power either through 'pressure group' politics or elections, cannot be urged to obey, or even to participate in elections, on the grounds that the division of power in our society is a fair compromise. If they do not participate in elections, neither of the special reasons for obedience peculiar to a democratic form of government will be applicable.

This conclusion is a ground for dissatisfaction with the state of affairs described by the writers we have been considering. The price that must be paid for our form of democracy is not just the elimination of self-development through participation, as other writers have argued. I think it possible that the weakness of the arguments for obedience, as they apply to Western democracies, is a factor in the amount of disobedience which now meets controversial decisions in many of these societies. As populations become increasingly educated and politically sophisticated, they, or at least a significant minority of them, see that the classical democratic rhetoric used by politicians and advocates of 'law and order' no longer applies to the political system responsible for the decisions to which they are opposed. They see that the pluralist system is not a fair compromise, and that elections between two dominant parties do not give equal opportunities for dissenting opinions —especially when the parties agree on controversial issues. Dr. Spock is only one among many who, although supporters of democracy, no longer feel obliged to accept the verdict of a decision-procedure which falls well short of the democratic ideal.

In 1956, Robert Dahl concluded his *Preface to Democratic Theory* by praising Americans for their contribution to the art of democratic government. He said of the American system: '. . . so long as the social prerequisites of democracy are substantially intact in this country, it appears to be a relatively efficient system for reinforcing agreement, encouraging moderation, and maintaining social peace . . .'[1] Looking back over the years since that was written, though the social prerequisites have remained substantially intact, we are unlikely to think so highly of the pacifying nature of the American political system.[2] Social peace is a matter of degree. America may not be in a state of civil war, but it has hardly been peaceful. Nor does the political system seem to reinforce agreement or encourage moderation very successfully. It is particularly significant that disobedience now is often directed at quite minor issues, not just those issues, like nuclear disarmament or the continuation of the war in Vietnam, about which it can be said that the evil against which the disobedience is directed is so

[1] p. 151.
[2] It is worth noting, though, that the late sixties and early seventies have not really had much more than the usual amount of political violence, judged by the standards of American life over the last 150 years. It is by comparison with the exceptionally peaceful period just before Dahl wrote that the period since has seemed so turbulent. See the *Report of the National Commission on the Causes and Prevention of Violence* (Bantam Books, New York, 1970), p. xxix.

great as to outweigh even democratic reasons for obeying the law. Of course, one cannot rule out the possibility that disrespect for law is a passing phase, or that those who engage in disobedience, especially on less important issues, are fundamentally undemocratic, or perhaps just muddle-headed. But if, on examination, this does not seem to be the case, and disobedience continues to be a serious problem, we should begin to consider seriously the possibility that the basis of political obligation in Western democracies is in need of reconstruction—or perhaps I should say, in need of construction, for there probably never has been a large-scale society with a satisfactory basis of political obligation. The need for such a basis, however, increases with the increasing political awareness of the population.

Should disobedience continue to grow, the failure of modern forms of democracy to generate the democratic reasons for obedience which would exist under a political system more nearly approximating to our model democratic society could appear so important that some effort to alter the form of our democracy in this direction has to be made. What would such a political system be like? A number of different political systems could satisfy the requirements of democratic obligation. The nature of our model suggests that these requirements will most easily be met in small groups, and this points towards political decentralization, and a devolution of power to local communities. Whether this is possible in societies as complex as ours is a moot point. Short of a radical change of this kind, there are various devices which might help to counteract the inegalitarian distribution of power in modern democracies. I have already suggested that a procedure by which a referendum could be called on any issue, if a certain number of electors requested it, would reduce the need for disobedience because it would be a way of putting an issue to the majority for reconsideration, and would speedily indicate the majority's view. At the same time, of course, it would make it possible for ordinary people to take a political initiative, without having to work through oligarchical parties, and would be a means of reaching decisions in which, apart from inequalities in the means of influencing people, everyone has an equal say.

Another obvious way to remedy one source of inequality of power would be to reform the internal structure of the major political parties so that they become genuinely democratic. In view of the tendency of large organizations to become oligarchical even when, as in the case of the British Labour Party, they have a democratic constitution, special care would need to be taken to prevent the leadership assuming a dominant position. This would require not only provisions for frequent rotation of positions within the party, but also a different spirit of equality among members, and a sense of the importance of maintaining this equality.

Finally, there is the question of reform of the electoral system. There is no doubt that the simple majority system used to elect the British House of Commons and the American House of Representatives has prevented alternative points of view from growing into significant political forces. Abstractly considered, proportional representation gives voters a more nearly equal share in the choice of representatives. It would thus remove one important source of inequality in the British and American political systems. Nor is it always associated with unstable government, as is sometimes said—the Scandinavian democracies, Switzerland, Belgium, and the Netherlands all combine stable government and proportional systems of representation.[1] Admittedly, whether a political system satisfies the requirements of democratic obligation is only one of several criteria by which political systems should be judged,

[1] See E. Lakeman, *How Democracies Vote: A Study of Majority and Proportional Electoral Systems* (3rd ed. Faber and Faber, London, 1970).

and so it may be argued—though I would not agree—that proportional representation has disadvantages which outweigh the advantages in terms of greater political equality. Whether we think this or the other reforms I have tentatively suggested worth experimenting with will no doubt depend partly on how serious a problem disobedience is in the future. This, in turn, will depend not only on the nature of our institutions, which were, after all, basically unchanged throughout the obedient fifties and the less obedient sixties, but also on the issues that arise. Racial discrimination and the war in Vietnam have done more to promote disobedience in the United States than all the defects of American political institutions.

CONCLUDING SUMMARY

WE have completed the task set at the beginning of this book: the examination of the view that if a system of government is democratic this vitally affects our obligation to obey laws emanating from that system. In carrying out this examination the preliminary conclusions reached in Part I have received a number of qualifications. It may therefore be helpful if I briefly restate the position at which we have finally arrived.

In a model democratic society, there would be important reasons for obeying the law which do not exist in other forms of government. Apart from the general consideration that any preference we have for one form of government over another is a reason for obeying the laws of the preferred form of government, there are two special reasons for obedience which are peculiar to democracy. The first is based on the fact that a democratic society, in which all have equal power and there is no tendency for the majority to treat the minority with less than equal consideration, is a fair compromise between competing, otherwise irresolvable, claims to power. The second stems from the fact that participating in a decision-procedure, alongside others participating in good faith, gives rise to an obligation to act as if one had consented to be bound by the result of the decision-procedure. So long as the participation is voluntary, actual consent is not required, but an express public refusal so to be bound would mean that participation, if still permitted, would not give rise to any obligation to obey the result.

These reasons for obeying laws in a democracy apply only

when no rights essential to the functioning of a fair compromise decision-procedure have been infringed. Among such rights are the well-known democratic rights of free speech, free association, the right to vote, and so on. The infringement of other rights, not essential to the functioning of a fair compromise decision-procedure, however, does not affect the force of the reasons for obedience.

There remain some forms of limited disobedience which do not run counter to the democratic reasons for obedience. Disobedience designed to gain publicity for a point of view which has not received a fair hearing, and disobedience aimed at inducing reconsideration of a decision, are compatible with fair compromise, and may assist in restoring a fair compromise when a basically equal decision-procedure is not working properly. Normally such disobedience ought to be non-violent and those disobeying ought to accept the legal penalties. There is nothing special about disobedience based on conscience which allows the 'conscientious objector' to ignore the democratic reasons for obeying the law.

Although our investigation had, up to this point, suggested that there is a great deal of truth in the view that there are much stronger reasons for obeying the law in a democratic society than in a non-democratic society, when we sought to transfer this conclusion from a model democratic society to the sort of society in which we live, we found less truth in it. The modern form of 'Western democracy', as described by leading political theorists favourable to it, is not a fair compromise between competing groups. Although more diverse and more numerous groups influence decisions than in a dictatorship, some groups have less than an equal share of influence, while many people are not effectively represented by groups at all. Elections, it is generally agreed, do not rectify this inequality. For groups and individuals with less than an equal say in decisions, the argument for obedience based on fair compromise does not apply, and the argument from participation, while still applicable to those who vote, is undermined by the absence of a sufficient reason, for many dissenters, for participating in elections.

AN ILLUSTRATION: DISOBEDIENCE IN
NORTHERN IRELAND

IN this book I have discussed, in general terms, the conditions under which disobedience for political purposes may be justifiable, and the forms which justifiable disobedience may take. I have, however, been able to say very little about the application of these principles in particular cases. This, I have frequently said, is a matter for judgement, taking all the relevant facts of the situation into account. To discuss these matters in general terms is, many people think, the most that can be done by a political philosopher—in fact, some philosophers define their province so narrowly that to discuss substantive issues at all is already to go beyond it. While, obviously, I disagree with the stricter of these conceptions of the role of the philosopher, I accept the view that it is asking too much of political philosophers to expect them to put forward simple guidelines for the application of their conclusions to particular situations. On the other hand, it has occurred to me when reading books on political obligation and similar topics that it would be useful if the author would give some indication—if not guidelines, then an illustration—of how his conclusions are to be applied. The following discussion of disobedience in Northern Ireland is intended to serve this purpose.

As a preface to what follows, I should say that I make no claim to be an expert on the situation in Northern Ireland. I have no first-hand knowledge of the situation, nor have I made a very intensive study of it. I have chosen Northern Ireland rather than the better-known example of disobedience against racial discrimination in the American South because in the latter case there is the complication that, as a result of the existence of the United States Constitution, to which there is no parallel in Northern Ireland, much 'disobedience' in the South was a protest against laws that were never legally valid. Otherwise, disobedience in Northern Ireland and in the South raise very similar questions. I did not choose the other prominent instance of disobedience, against the war in Vietnam, because this issue, though complex with respect to matters of fact, seems to raise few of the philosophical issues discussed in this book. Once one rejects the view that the war was necessary for the defence of South Vietnam against Communist aggression inspired by the North Vietnamese, then the death and destruction inflicted on the Vietnamese has been so monstrous that if there were any reasonable hope of stopping the war by means of disobedience, the need to stop it would override any democratic obligations to obey which might count against disobedience in other situations.

In the following discussion I have tried to rely on facts rather than opinion (except at the final stage at which there is no substitute for opinion) and preferably facts which are not likely to be disputed. Most of my information can be found in newspapers and in such sources as the *Sunday Times* Insight Team's report, *Ulster*.[1] I have made no attempt to deal with all aspects of the issues involved, but have selected those aspects which seemed most usefully to illustrate points discussed in the course of this book.

There are several strands of illegal activity interwoven in the crisis which developed in Northern Ireland in the late 1960s. Most prominent have been the activities of the Irish Republican Army, whose bombings and shootings have caused approximately 400 deaths and damage estimated at

[1] Penguin Books, Harmondsworth, 1972.

£50,000,000, between 1968 and the time of writing (July 1972). Illegal I.R.A. activities did not begin in 1968; there has been a sporadic campaign of resistance since Ireland was partitioned in 1922. Although the I.R.A. has sometimes tried to justify its actions in terms of the defence of an oppressed minority, it has never accepted the legitimacy of partition or the Ulster Government, and there can be little doubt that its aim is not an end to discrimination, but the unification of Ireland. The I.R.A. does not regard its illegal activities as disobedience *within* a political system, democratic or otherwise; its leaders claim that they are at war with the British Army, which they regard as a foreign army of occupation on Irish soil. Whatever the justification for this position, it is a position which puts the I.R.A. campaign outside the scope of this book, which is concerned with the justification of disobedience rather than war.

A second strand of illegal action in Ulster is the violence and intimidation to which Catholics, particularly in Catholic districts of Belfast and Londonderry, have been subjected by militant Protestants. This too goes back to a period well before the flare-up of the sixties. Protestant mobs attacked Catholics in 1920 and 1935; Protestant violence has ranged from breaking windows to the 1966 Malvern Street murders. This Protestant illegality also falls outside the scope of our inquiry, simply because no justification, or at least no moral justification, has been offered for it at all; nor can I see how any justification could be attempted. Protestant violence of this kind is hooliganism or religious persecution. No theory of political obligation is required to determine whether such conduct is wrong.

It is with the third strand of disobedience in Ulster that we are concerned. This is disobedience, often described as civil disobedience, by Catholics who claim that they have not been treated as equals by the Protestant majority. This third strand is the campaign which began under the auspices of the Northern Ireland Civil Rights Association in 1968, a campaign that crossed the boundary between legal demonstration and civil disobedience on 5 October 1968, when a march was held in Londonderry in defiance of a ministerial ban. This campaign raises a number of the issues which have been discussed in this book.

The first question to be asked is: was the position of Catholics in Northern Ireland prior to October 1968 such as would justify disobedience? This question can be broken down into two questions: was the Catholic minority a victim of persistent discrimination? If so, was disobedience an appropriate means of seeking redress?

Earlier in this book, when I put forward the view that a decision-procedure in which every member had an equal say was a fair compromise, I conceded that there could be circumstances in which despite formal equality there was no fair compromise because a permanent majority was using its power to disregard the interests of the minority. I said then that to show that this was the case it would be necessary to show, not an isolated unfair decision, but a persistent pattern of unfairness. I also said that it was a matter of judgement in each situation whether acts of unfairness constituted a pattern of unfairness, and that as a safeguard against too much disobedience one might require the pattern of unfairness to be 'unmistakably clear', rather than merely probable.[1] I think an examination of the position of the Catholic minority in the years preceding the events of 1968 shows that, though judgement may be required, this does not introduce too great a degree of subjectivity into questions of political obligation, for there are situations in which a pattern of unfairness is unmistakably clear.

To reveal a persistent pattern of discrimination against Catholics in Northern Ireland, it will suffice to examine the situation in three areas: employment, housing, and local

[1] pp. 42–5 above.

government, while bearing in mind that about one-third of the population of the province is Catholic.[1]

In employment, the most notable area of discrimination was in work under the control of the Government of Northern Ireland and local governments. At Stormont (the Ulster Parliament building) discrimination in government employment was so much the norm that Protestants would occasionally accuse their ministers of employing Catholics. Ministers were usually able to rebut the charge satisfactorily. Thus in 1925 the Minister of Agriculture, defending himself against such an accusation, said: 'I have 109 officials and so far as I know, four of them are Roman Catholics, three of whom were civil servants turned over to me, whom I had to take on when we began.' Fermanagh, one of the six counties which comprise the province of Northern Ireland, has a population almost equally divided between Catholic and Protestant; of the 370 people employed by Fermanagh County Council at one time in the late sixties, 332 were Protestant, and none of the Catholic employees held senior positions. In the city of Londonderry there were, in 1966, 14,325 Catholics and only 9,235 Protestants: in the same year, all the heads of the City Council departments were Protestant, and of 177 salaried employees, only thirty-two were Catholic. Among private concerns, the largest single employer of labour was in 1972 the Belfast shipyard. It employed 10,000 workers: 9,600 were Protestant.

Housing in Ulster, as throughout Britain, is to a considerable extent provided by local councils. Discrimination in this field shows itself in at least three ways. First, in some places, Dungannon for instance, the Council provided better houses in Protestant areas than in Catholic areas, the same rent securing forty-two extra square feet of space for Protestants. Secondly, it was easier for Protestants to obtain council houses.

[1] The facts on which the following is based are drawn from *Ulster*, pp. 29–37.

Two-thirds of the houses built by Fermanagh County Council between 1945 and 1969 went to Protestants, despite the county's balanced population. Thirdly, councils refused to build houses for Catholics outside Catholic areas, which meant that these areas became badly overcrowded. This practice also had advantages for Protestants in terms of the third main area of discrimination, local politics.

Local politics was the key to the Protestant supremacy in council employment and council housing. While a Protestant majority in Stormont, the parliamentary assembly representing the whole province, was to be expected in view of the numerical supremacy of Protestants in Northern Ireland as a whole, Protestants also managed, by blatant gerrymandering, to control local government in areas with evenly distributed populations, or even, as in Londonderry, with substantial Catholic majorities. Fermanagh County Council, in the late sixties, consisted of thirty-five Unionists, i.e. Protestants, and seventeen non-Unionists. In Londonderry the classic technique of putting all Catholic areas into one huge ward produced a Borough Council with eight Catholic councillors and twelve Protestants. This pattern was repeated in many other areas.

Evidence of this sort, I think, constitutes an overwhelming case for saying that Catholics in Northern Ireland were an oppressed minority. There is almost nothing that can be said in justification of these inequalities. It is true that when Northern Ireland was first established Catholics wanted no part in the new province, and in many cases refused government appointments even when they were offered, but attitudes had changed since the twenties, and if the Unionists had made any effort to deal equitably with Catholics, there can be little doubt that a reasonable approximation to equality could have been achieved well before the late sixties.

Taking it as established, then, that there was a persistent

pattern of unfairness in the treatment of the Catholic minority by the Protestant majority, was disobedience an appropriate means of seeking redress in October 1968? As I have suggested in this book, and as others have also urged, when legal procedures are available, an attempt to seek redress of grievances by legal means should be made first, and disobedience resorted to only if there is no reasonable prospect of achieving redress by legal means.

In Northern Ireland, although there had been occasional protests at injustice since partition, the reform movement which eventually led to disobedience can be said to have begun in 1964, when the Campaign for Social Justice was founded.[1] In the succeeding years, greater interest was taken, especially in Britain, in the question of justice for Catholics in Northern Ireland. In 1966, for instance, the *Sunday Times* published an examination of discrimination in Ulster entitled 'John Bull's Political Slum'. As that article suggested, however, Ulster's ruling Protestants were making no real effort to end discrimination, and it seemed unlikely that they would do so unless strongly pressed by the British Government. Although under the Government of Ireland Act the British Government retains supreme authority in Northern Ireland, at that time the Labour Government was adhering to the doctrine of preceding British Governments, that Northern Ireland is best left to look after itself.

A further step in the campaign for reform by legal means was the founding, in 1967, of the Northern Ireland Civil Rights Association, an organization with moderate liberal aims, modelled on the National Council for Civil Liberties in England. For about a year the Civil Rights Association confined itself to dealing with individual complaints. In June 1968, however, it held a peaceful and legal march to publicize a particularly blatant instance of Protestant bias in the alloca-

[1] See *Ulster*, pp. 41 ff.

tion of council housing. It then announced a march to take place in Londonderry, as a protest against the inegalitarian distribution of power in that city. Shortly before the march which was to take place on 5 October, William Craig, then Northern Ireland Minister for Home Affairs, banned all marches in Londonderry. The campaign of disobedience began when the Civil Rights Association decided to defy this ban.

Was this decision justified? Legal means of achieving reform had not been exhausted; on the other hand, more than four years of normal political activity had failed to make significant progress, except in individual cases. The ban on the Londonderry march denied to Catholics one of the means—normally legal—of campaigning for reform. The first march sponsored by the Civil Rights Association had been successful in drawing attention to injustice. Now the Protestant Government was seeking to prevent the next step in what had been, and might have continued to be, a legal reform movement.

Before one can decide whether defiance of the ban was justified, one must ask what reason the Government gave for issuing the order prohibiting marches. The ban was issued after police reports that the march was likely to result in violence, these reports being based on the fact that a Protestant organization, the Apprentice Boys of Derry,[1] had announced, shortly before the Civil Rights march was due, that they proposed to hold a march on the same day, and over the same route, as the planned Civil Rights march. It seems to me that the relevant question here is: was the ban, and the situation that led to it, an exceptional and short-term phenomenon, or was the same thing likely to happen to other proposed Civil Rights marches in future? In other words, was the clash of Catholic and Protestant marches a genuine coincidence, carrying with

[1] Consisting not of real apprentice boys, but of Protestants honouring the apprentice boys who closed the gates of Londonderry against the army of James II.

it a real danger of violence, but unlikely to recur, or was it a Protestant attempt to prevent Catholics marching against injustice which was likely to be repeated whenever Catholics attempted to protest? If the former was the case, the ban was not an attempt to prevent Catholics being heard, and the right course would seem to be to obey the ban and re-schedule the march for another occasion. If, on the other hand, the clash was deliberate and likely to recur on any other occasion, then disobedience would seem to be justified, either on this occasion or on a future occasion.

On this question, a judge appointed by the British Government to inquire into these events had this to say: 'We are satisfied . . . that this proposed [Protestant] procession was not a genuine 'annual' event, and we regard the proposal to hold it at the precise time indicated as merely a threat to counter demonstrate by opponents of the Civil Rights march.'[1] The *Sunday Times* Insight Team disagrees: it believes that there were longstanding plans to hold an Apprentice Boys' march on that weekend. But the Insight Team agrees that at the time this was regarded 'merely as a Protestant counter-ploy'.[2] Since we are interested in Northern Ireland for illustrative purposes, and not to sit in judgement on the leaders of the Civil Rights Association, we need not try to settle this issue. It is enough to see what conclusions follow from the two possible ways of looking at the facts. We can perhaps add, though, that if in a case like this there is any doubt in one's mind about what the true facts are, little is lost, and the need for disobedience may be removed, if one gives the government the benefit of the doubt the first time, and waits to see what happens on another occasion.

One set of circumstances in which disobedience would be justified, then, can be seen from our illustration. In a political

[1] From the report by Lord Cameron, quoted in *Ulster*, p. 51.
[2] Ibid. p. 51.

system which does not operate as a fair compromise, when legal means of achieving reform have proven unsuccessful over a number of years, and when there are long-term restrictions on normally legal means of campaigning for reform, disobedience will, I believe, be justified. Even if Catholics had participated in elections in Northern Ireland (and there would, in fact, have been little reason for them to do so, under the electoral boundaries of the time) I would think that the quasi-consensual obligation arising from participation would in these circumstances have been overridden, particularly as the disobedience in question was really disobedience designed to publicize injustice, rather than to alter by force a decision taken by the decision-procedure.

Our discussion of disobedience in Northern Ireland has now served its main purpose, which was to describe actual circumstances in which the question of whether to disobey arose, and attempt to decide whether disobedience was justified. There are, however, some secondary points about disobedience which I will also try to illustrate briefly in relation to the course of events in Northern Ireland.

One practical lesson that emerges from Northern Ireland is the ease with which disobedience can escalate into counter-disobedience and violence. The Londonderry march of 5 October 1968 ended in violence. According to Lord Cameron's report there were extremists present who wished to provoke a confrontation with the police. If so, they had no difficulty in doing so, for the march ended with the police batoning the leaders of the march, an action which was, as the same report said, 'wholly without justification or excuse'.[1] Later, Protestant groups practised their own form of disobedience, gathering in large numbers with sticks and more sinister weapons on the routes of protest marches. In this way, they forced the cancellation of a march in Armagh on 30 November, and on 4 January

[1] Ibid., p. 52

1969 brutally attacked a legal march outside Londonderry.[1] Ultimately, as is well-known, the escalation of violence led to the resurgence of the I.R.A. and the movement for justice and reform was pushed out of the spotlight.

Another important issue raised by the Ulster situation is how much time a government should be given to reform itself once a commitment to reform has been given. On 22 November 1968, only six days after a second illegal, but this time non-violent march in Londonderry, the Prime Minister of Northern Ireland announced a plan for reform which met the main Catholic demands, including means for ensuring justice in housing and local government, and the speedy replacement of the gerrymandered Londonderry Borough Council by a Development Commission. This looked like a spectacular success for the reform movement, and the Londonderry Council was replaced within three months; but three years later there had still been no effective reform of housing and local government.[2] The escalation of violence provided the Unionists with an excellent reason/excuse (how one regards it will depend on one's point of view) for failing to press ahead with reforms as energetically as it might otherwise have done. Should there have been a more concerted effort by Catholics to calm the situation down, once the reform package was announced? I am inclined to think there should have been, though it is easier to suggest moderation than to practise it, and Catholics did have some reason to fear that if the pressure on Unionists eased too much the reforms might be quietly forgotten.

Finally, the fate of the campaign for reform shows clearly the importance, when practising disobedience for publicity purposes, of making it very plain that the disobedience is not an attempt to coerce the majority; and similarly, when one is disobeying to protest against specific injustices, of making it

[1] Ibid., pp. 61, 66.   [2] Ibid., p. 59.

plain that one is not attacking the political system as a whole. These dangers were especially great in Northern Ireland, because the Catholics had at first refused to accept the partition of Ireland and the political system of Northern Ireland. The failure of Ulster Protestants to understand that the Civil Rights Association was not a challenge to the separate political existence of Northern Ireland was influential in the decision to ban the Londonderry march, and in the violence with which Protestant mobs attacked civil rights marchers on other occasions. Thus Craig, the Minister responsible for the ban, dismissed the Civil Rights Association as 'bogus and made up of people who see in unrest a chance to renew a campaign of violence'—a view which the Cameron report decisively rejected.[1] In the opinion of the *Sunday Times* Insight Team:

The beginning of the subsequent [i.e. after the I.R.A. had become virtually extinct in the early sixties] story of Ulster is a fatal error by the ruling Protestants. It was to mistake the Civil Rights movement of the sixties for an attack on the State of Ulster itself. Thus, by choice of the ruling élite, the energy of the reformist impulse has been made to shake the foundations of society.[2]

It may be that nothing Catholics could have done would have convinced Protestants that Catholic objectives could be met within the framework of a separate Northern Ireland. Nevertheless, there is at least a possibility that a more disciplined campaign, conducted along the lines of the campaigns of Gandhi or Martin Luther King, and including readiness to accept the legal penalties for disobedience and willingness to behave passively in the face of violence could have shown the Protestants that they were making a potentially disastrous mistake. In saying this I am aware that, as always in a case like this, it is easier to advocate restraint than to practise it in the face of violence and provocation.

[1] Ibid., pp. 46–7. [2] Ibid., p. 27.

INDEX